The Little Religions of Paris

THE LITTLE RELIGIONS OF PARIS

by

Jules Bois

Essay
(1894)

Triad Press
Fox Lake, IL

The Little Religions of Paris
by Jules Bois (1894)

Translated by Tau Phosphoros

First English-language edition
Published October, 2022

ISBN: 978-1-946814-08-1

Triad Press, LLC
123 S. U.S. 12
#33
Fox Lake, IL 60020

Table of Contents

INTRODUCTION

We have disdained too much until now the little sects with strange worship with which Paris teems, a new Byzantium. They are usually treated with fantastic documents or a summary criticism. Certain of them remain profoundly ignored. But a faith apparently in vain, when it is sincere, is to be scoffed at only with caution. All these sects, even irrational ones, touch on those troubling problems of our destiny in the beyond and on our relationship with the Invisible. The woman is celebrated here with a great respect and a charming sweetness; worship, rendered to the ancestors, to the dead, and to those that we do not see, is fervent here unto superstition; and the miracle affects an exaggerated, but consoling frequency. The majority are touching, some have a spice of terror, all are picturesque. Let us study them like sanctuary trinkets, inoffensive monsters, old-fashioned or yet too childish, and we will delight that they bring into our too skeptical society a revival of mysticism or at least a slightly noble cause for distraction.

To these studies on the little religions of Paris, the *Figaro* granted me a hospitality which earned me a considerable number of letters; they have convinced me to push further my inquiry, here are the results.

THE LAST PAGANS

I have made my pilgrimage place Sorbonne, at the pagan house, decorated by the most beautiful bas-reliefs from the Greek temples. It is here that dreams and works M. Louis Ménard, incontestably the most venerable of the adorers of Olympian Jupiter.

M. Louis Ménard held a cigarette out to me while praying me to sit, and as I refused it:

"You are wrong! This is henceforth the sole homage that we make to the gods, in offering them a little smoke; which is worthy of their implacable essence."

And the mysterious scholar tamped a sacrificial pipe which would soon satisfy the nostrils of some invisible king of the Ether.

I look around me. Despite the books which are displayed, the papers and letters piled up, the studio has an indefinable serene allure, recalling the bright sanctuaries of the Olympian divinities.

"Alas! We are indeed fallen," continued M. Louis Ménard. "This pipe alone makes us superior to the ancients."

On the walls, some old cloths become faded; there, endlessly, this solitary poured out for himself alone that soul of heroic idyll that Hesiod, Theocritus, and Virgil fed from the most exquisite remembrances of dead centuries. But the gods themselves inhabit the studio. Virile Beauty, personified in Jupiter, faces Apollo, the eternal youth. Venus looks, in turning away a little, at Diana; for love has always feared chastity. Here, M. Louis Ménard is seated under the bust of Homer, arranging family letters, full of discussions on the life and great feats of Heracles, of Tiphaon, and of that prudent Athena.

With his long hair, grey here and there, which frames his triangular face, where his eyes shine like the torches of the mysteries at their initiations, the hierophant poet appears to me similar to those sages of Alexandira who explained to their disciples under the colonnades the legends of the external forces and the miracles of the daemons.

"I do not know any priest," this modern pagan asserts to me; "my worship to the gods is wholly interior."

"They have assured me that before reading Sophocles you sacrifice doves to Aphrodite. Here is the anecdote: You wanted one day to teach Greek to the sonorous poet José-Maria de Heredia. At the moment of opening Sophocles, you suddenly took out two turtle-doves from your pocket... 'No one truly knew Greek,' you say, 'unless, before applying himself to it, he offered the entrails of these birds to the charming Venus. We will both eat the rest.' But M. de Heredia wrinkled his brow and responded with an unpardonable skepticism: 'My friend, I do not like pigeon.' "

"That is not exact," replied my subtle interlocutor while smiling. "I would not wring the neck of a chicken, and only the demands of my health prohibit me from being vegetarian... At the time of the first sacrifices, when they led the steer to the altar strewn with sacred herbs, the animal snapped up this prey with an eager tongue. Then the indignant pontiff threw an axe to the victim. The people who obscured the view of the blood, impeached the sacrificer; but he responded that only the axe was criminal and later it arises that the Axe was acquitted as not responsible... The sacrifices were a compromise between the gluttony of men and their terror at shedding blood."

"But you have prayed the Immortals?"

"I have prayed Hermes, the god of unexpected windfalls, and he has had me encounter only pencils and hair-pins; however, I have rendered him the great service of revealing to the moderns his true meaning: *twilight*."

"The pagan cult disappeared then all of a sudden?"

"I am perhaps the last who, mystically, renders homage to the gods of Homer. During the renaissance - M. Despois has related - there was a renewal of paganism. The long discussions of the Council of Trente permitted certain cardinals to smile while thinking in their soul that the faith in the powers of Olympus cannot be eradicated. But the Jewish idea of unity has triumphed. In order to recreate a popular paganism, it would be necessary to admit the plurality of causes, and that idea, descending into the masses, gives birth to new legends... In the main, however, polytheism exists, it is the worship of the dead..."

"Spiritism?"

"No, I think that the spiritists are mistaken, but I can believe that those who were alive intervene in our affairs in order to protect us"

"Indeed, but I have trouble understanding how one may worship the gods who are themselves without form, who do not exist."

"But the gods have a body. Artemis, the huntress, is the crescent of the moon, similar to a bow. Apollo is the sun. If both preside over death, it is because men disappear by the accumulation of days and nights. The Jewish god himself, Jehovah, is the simoom. Whoever has glanced through, in Hesiod, the struggle of Jupiter and the Titans, it is quickly seen that it is a tempest that he has wished to describe."

"Have you never been tempted to become Christian?"

"They have tried to convert me. Here is how. I had accompanied to the cemetery the funeral procession of a friend. There I encountered a young and unknown woman who spoke praises to me of the one who had died with all the sacraments of the Church. I responded to her: 'Happy are those who have faith.' These words struck her. She wrote me a letter where a very lucid intelligence was revealed: 'It has seemed to me,' she told me, 'that there was some sadness in these words, and that, close to the tomb of the one who was without doubt your friend, the great thoughts of death and eternity had troubled you.' At the same time this young lady recommended to me some pious books. I returned them to her while thanking her, and I assured her that I believe in Christ like her, since I acknowledge all the gods...

"Look, if you want proof, here is a letter that I addressed to my mother, while she congratulated me, believing me returned to orthodox beliefs:

... "I prefer to live in communication with the entire population of the spirits. You will tell me that this is polytheism. This is true, but Christ has said: 'My kingdom is not of this world' and with good reason, for he is the God of the inner world. The exterior world also has its gods. The sun, the stars, the elements, and those that the physicists call the forces of nature are redoubtable powers... But there has to be magnetic or magical powers to direct these forces. They say in vain that the laws of nature are immutable: between the thunderbolt and the house upon which it falls, one can place a lightning-rod. Who knows if such a formula of exorcism, such a prayer has not an analogous force? I am convinced that the energetic prayer of a mother may be placed between her child and death like a lightning-rod. I am reminded of a bullet which passed through my hair, at the hour when I was prayed for, and I believe that without this prayer the bullet would have been lower. Who knows if prayer cannot even erase accomplished facts...? Often when we dream of a misfortune and then we thank the Gods for waking us; who knows if more than once these misfortunes were not quite real? Dream and reality are not so different that the supreme powers cannot sometimes change reality into a dream. But here is an entirely mystical idea, and if one believes it in an absolute manner one would become mad..."

M. Louis Ménard interrupted himself by smiling and rummaging through some other yellowed bundles from where he extracted an amusing controversy; the tournament of a brother and sister, of Louis and Anne for and against the gods of pagan art, for and against the saints of Christian art.

First the letter from Louis:

"My dear Anna,

"This morning I have been allowed to penetrate into the council of the great gods of the earth, an honor which is accorded to me from time to time; I listened to them who told me: 'You do not know the news, Anna Ménard scorns us, she finds our histories *amusing*, that is her expression!' - 'Has she really held this language?' asked Venus, 'I have never heard it, soothed as I was by the rustling of the wings of my doves. Oh! Really! If men scorn us, all the worse for them. Since they have broken our magnificent statues, the sculptors today make nothing but "hotch-potch." Talk to me of the famous Milo!' - Then Jupiter who gathers the distant clouds responded: 'You have reason, daughter of the foam; what the physicists of today call law, I do not know why the attraction. The mortals no longer know how to draw; let this be their punishment. The other gods do what they want, as for me despite the blasphemes of Anna, I wish to continue to shed my celestial dew upon the fertile earth.' - 'You have spoken wisely, father of the gods and men,' replied the divine Sun, 'what does the incense of the mortals matter to us? Is it not sufficient for us to hear each dawn the universal hymn of the rebirth of nature? And you, Venus with the sweet smile, what does it matter if men forget you? The songs of the bird of the woods respond in concert with the stars when the pearls of your hair while falling unto the prairie cover it with a carpet of flowers.'

" 'But' Minerva then said, 'why doesn't Anna read the poems of Homer? It seems to me that this would give her less absurd ideas on Olympus and its inhabitants! - 'One fears that she should become as learned as you, my daughter,' said Jupiter; 'one finds that I have seen to give her too fine an education. Anna's parents, in examining her stockings, have believed to notice that they took on a most alarming bluish hue and have declared that the woman had to remain plunged into ignorance.' Amen."

During this reading, I gazed at the friezes of the Parthenon reproduced on the wall; then my eyes stopped lower down on a Madonna painting engarlanded with flowers.

"And the response?" I asked.
"Here it is:"
"My dear Louis,

"These last days I have been allowed to penetrate into the abode of the souls of the painters long since dead, and to hear their conversation. I heard Raphael who said: 'Do you not know the news? Louis Ménard has scorned us; he finds that we do not know how to draw. It is Venus who has put these ideas into his head. It appears that she has had the cheek to say before all of Olympus that since the *famous Milo* they make nothing but "hotch-potch" and Louis Ménard is eager to repeat these blasphemies.' - 'Has Louis really spoken in this way?' asked then Anglico de Fiesole. 'I have not heard it, occupied that I was with listening to the harmonious hymns of my angels. O my beautiful saints, it is then in vain that for so many ages, you pray kneeling with an unalterable fervor! Men insult us and scorn us. Now here we find you ugly and badly drawn.' - 'But,' said Leonardo de Vinci, 'our virgins have not ceased to be beautiful, they do not even wince in hearing said that they are ugly, for their sweet beauty is above human judgments.' - 'You have spoken wisely,' replied Raphael, 'they are not angered by the blasphemes of men, for their glances turn only to the earth in order to shed there their blessings and divine inspirations.' - 'That is very good!' said Michaelangelo, who until then had not opened his mouth, 'but I think that if Louis Ménard had studied our work sometime, he would find that we make anything but "hotch-potch," and I wish to feed him, in regards to us, some ideas a little less absurd.' - Amen."

"Have you recruited any disciples?" I questioned.

"Never, or rather one - Lamé... This was dreadful, he died mad. One night he came to my home. 'I have just prayed to Brahma all day,' he told me, 'and he has revealed to me that you are the Holy Spirit and X... the Word.' - 'You

8

do me too great an honor,' I responded, 'but I think that it would be better of you to go lie down. 'He replied tranquilly: 'You are deceiving yourself, if you believe me insane. I conform to your symbolism. Are you not the Holy Spirit, who has made me discover the meaning of the religious myths, and is not X... the Word, he who teaches me Sanskrit?' I insisted that he rest himself. The next day I warned his friends, but when I returned to visit him, it was already too late. He had thrown himself through a window, writing: 'Now I am like the gods. I crossed my arms and launched myself into eternity!'

"Droz did not want to believe in this extraordinary death: ' I know well that he was mad,' he told me, 'but I believed that it was like you.' "

We can rest easy, M. Louis Ménard will never be mad. He has withstood the reading of the Neoplaonists, and he loves his books too much to throw himself from his fifth floor. Furthermore, the prudent Athena counsels him and keeps him. He would not go as far as these young men whose anonymity I will not reveal, and that I have caught having upon their white vestments a panther skin in order to render to the invisible nymphs inhabiting the lake of the wood of Boulogne the worship which was their due at Eleusis. Among the letters I have still, M. François de Nion, who I suspect, although a good Christian, has reserved a corner of his garden of Chatou to the subtle Dionysos; neo-paganism has its most noble prophetess in Madame Adam, recently converted to the ideas of reincarnation that occultism professes; and, I have no doubt, Miss Holmès, whose heart belongs to the Olympian divinities, would be disposed towards writing to the Triumphal Ode of paganism, which renews itself only to better die.[1]

THE SWEDENBORGIANS

At 12 Thouin street, a little temple with the allure of a synagogue... I am, it appears, at the "New Jerusalem" announced by the Apocalypse.

In a sort of bay painted in blue, the pulpit stands on a double staircase. Below, on a bare table, the Bible. Through these hours of a Sunday afternoon, I observe, in the midst of a ghostly silence that punctuates the sermon of the pastor, these pointed skulls of mysticism, sad and ardent eyes of anemic girls, mourning attire of widows, and, here and there, some melancholy children. All mutely recalling the stubborn faith and hopelessness of the sects of which this is but one.

His discourse ended, the pastor has seated himself and indicated the number of a canticle. Immediately, while new to me, hands flop whimsically to the right page of a book. And around me spread timid voices singing couplets of an evangelical idolism...

> O Jesus in the Manger
> Lead your happy flocks,
> Keep your cherished Church
> And tend us as your sheep.
> May all these children of light,
> Filled with your spirit of love,
> Carry themselves everywhere upon the earth,
> Until the hour of your return.

This milieu of trembling souls weighs on me and deceives me. My spirit bores holes in these cold barriers, and according to the method of the prophet, I evoke him himself, that Swedenborg whose works caused the giddiness of the great Balzac himself.

He appears to me in his rateem garb with multiple reflections, steel buttons, with his white necktie, his waistcoat closed and that decorative wig with powdered rolls on the sides, such as one may see in the antechamber of the Swedenborgian Library. Angelic and childlike mouth which always has a smile, having tasted heaven; but those nostrils wide as if in order to breathe the planetary ether, that powerful brow, those thin cheeks show the visionary whose energy created around him a world sprung from his faith. And I remember his candid conversation, while, during a substantial repast, a mysterious voice, suddenly, rose up in the corner of the room, saying, not without a biblical familiarity: "Do not eat so much!"

From then on, the one who was previously the minerologist, the physician, the mathematician, and the most extraordinary astronomer of Sweden, fasted and believed himself devoted to explaining to men, according to the law of correspondences, the inner meaning of the Scriptures. And no one accomplished this hypothetical duty more loyally. Barely fed on semolina mash with milk, in his bed chamber from where he emerged only for long voyages, he was unaware of day and night, maintaining a burning log in the fireplace and laboring as much as the angels dictated to him.

...And instead of that Huguenot Bible upon which the hand of the modern pastor of the New Jerusalem rested, he seemed to me to perceive as a column of light, slightly smoky with incense, the infinite pile of works of the Apostle, with their transcendent and bizarre titles, from *les délices de l'Amour conjugal et les voluptés de la folie de l'Amour scortatoire* to the *Traité du Cheval Blanc de l'Apocalypse.*

However, in recalling that from January 23 to November 11, 1748, he explored Mercury six times, Jupiter twenty-three times, Mars six times, Saturn three times, and the Moon once, reporting from these excursions a detailed account of the morals, landscapes, and populations of these planets, I was astonished before such miracles, devolved upon the one who denied all miracles, to find myself in such modest company in this obscure temple, as large as a bed chamber.

I am sure that the scientist M. Jules Soury, distiller of brains, would discover in this divine fool the mania of persecutions, since he attributed to demoniacal influence even unto his toothaches. However, in his visions of heaven and hell, Swedenborg, who energetically resisted being a mystic, remained naively human. In the image of Dante, did he not place his enemies in Gehenna and his intimates in paradise?

It is that, for this dreamer, the spiritual world resembles the material world, of which it becomes the cause and the life. The earth is the nursery and the symbol of Heaven and Hell. From the chrysalis of men, emerge the Spirits and the Angels. The Angels, glorious souls, deserve all praise, and Swedenborg chose them for his most frequent conversations. Now, every terrestrial man has around him no more the Angel of Good and the Angel of Evil of the Church - but two angels and two spirits: a celestial angel and an infernal spirit prowling around his intelligence, then an infernal spirit and a celestial angel assailing his heart.

...The singing continued... I was no longer in the little Church, I had wandered into the Heaven of

Swedenborg, and I relived the delights of this in comparable account: "At the end of several walkways, I caught sight of a garden occupying the middle of a grove. The gates were opened to me by a guardian. I asked him: 'What is the name of this garden?' He answered me: 'Adramandoni, or the delights of conjugal love.' I entered. Among the olive trees vines ran and hung, and below them flowered shrubs. In the middle of the garden a grass cirque where were seated his bands and wives, and also young men and virgins, two by two, in the middle of the cirque a small fountain spouted water by the sole force of its source. Two angels, vested in purple and sparkling, spoke to the couples of the origin of love and its delights... At the end of the talk, upon the head of some of them appeared crowns of flowers. They asked: 'Why is this?' And the angels answered: 'Those who have been crowned have understood most profoundly.'"

Chairs striking each other at my sides awakens me from my revery...They depart. I rub my eyes, believing to be a dupe of an illusion, for it seemed to me impossible that such a prodigious founder of religion was commemorated by so few adepts.

Then I remember the terrible word of Kant who, with respect to Swedenborg, wrote one day: "Formerly, they burned the prophets; today, it suffices to purge them." The world has heard the council of Kant.

I believe that M. Décembre, the learned pastor who gave the signal to depart by blessing us, hands extended, has himself been "purged" according to the precept of the great rationalist. This Swedenborgian is reasonable, all as if he were not Swedenborgian. On the third floor of the neighboring house, he confides to me, in his calm voice:

"Swedenborg is an exceptional case, and, for my part, I am far from accepting all of his visionary doctrine."

"But," said I, astonished, "Swedenborg has described heaven with the exactitude of a naturalistic novelist. Each has, up there, the apartment that he merits. (May it not be the same here below!) His houses are in precious stones and gold, the branches of the trees are in silver. All the angels have a mouth, ears, and a tongue like men, but the dialect of the peoples of hell are evil and produce the horror of a gnashing of teeth. In the Dark Empire, there are naught but caverns of wild beasts, ruins of towns after the fire, sterile deserts. The demons showing frightful faces, deprived of life. The ones have a resemblance to pitch, others appear burning like torches, several are hideous with pustules, varixes, and ulcers. Some of them reveal themselves only in a hairy or osseous form. The more fearful no longer have faces, they are: a tooth!"

M. Décembre, a little too biblical and protestant, smiled: "The patriarch of our Church, M. Human, would explain all this to you according to the symbolic meaning. I see, according to my lights, only the dreams or the nightmares of a genius; I barely agree with the prophet that the Africans think in a manner more spiritual than the others less pious, and that the Angels have a sex."

"You must, however," I interrupt, "appreciate as an artist this description that he gives us of the tortures of the debauched in the beyond: 'They have their garments rent,' he says, 'and their breeches drawn up to above the abdomen, around the chest, because they have no loins - the loins being reserved for conjugal love - but at the region of the lower abdomen begin the heels of their feet,' "

We then chat about the present state of the "New

Jerusalem":

"Despite our disdain of propaganda, it made true progress. We have opened up our library for the neighborhood children who, instead of running about in the streets, are instructed with us. Our great feasts, Noel, Easter, the Pentecost, are also for the children. After the service, the Lord's Supper, with, as unique prayer, the Decalogue and the Our Father, the last verse of which is: 'For it is to you that belongs the kingdom, the power, and the glory!' He also read there all the passages that Swedenborg had dedicated to the fraternal agape. Finally, the grown-ups satisfied, we have the children sing hymns, we distribute clothing to the poorest, to the others pastries and toys. To all, the good word. Swedenborg loved them so much, these little ones, of whom he said that after their death, they are going to dwell in the eyes of God!

"In France, the first disciples were - note this unforeseen particularity - under the Restoration, from the officers of the 23rd line. A priest of Notre Dame, the Abbé Agger, joined them. M. Le Boys des Guays, at first a judge, then subprefect, opened public worship at Saint-Arnaud, in 1837, after the Abbé Ledru, curé near Chartres, had preached, in a barn erected into a temple, the doctrines of the 'New Jerusalem." From Chartres and Saint-Amand, the Church emigrated to Paris.

"The disciples first gathered with M. Broussais, son of the celebrated professor at the faculty of medicine, then, after some peregrinations, Rue de Sommerard where was found a circulating book shop.

"Finally, the first temple was built at Paris. It is in that very place where you have come to hear the service, on this small street that the Pantheon, by its majesty, makes more discreet.

"In Paris, we are scarcely more than two hundred, but there are at least a million Swedenborgians in the world. At the Congress of Chicago, our representatives have been more numerous than those of the other religions. Among them are women, for in the theological domain, we accord them a large place."

"Would it not be with respect to them," I interrupted, "that Swedenborg pronounced this memorable phrase: 'I have seen in the heavens angels who wore hats'? It seems to me that this is indeed a mystical definition of the woman."

"Perhaps," replied the amiable M. Décembre while smiling, "but the practices of spiritism are repugnant to us, which they love a little too much, and we have nothing in common with the Free Swedenborgians."

I went down Rue Thouin with the orthodox, I returned on Rue d'Amsterdam with the heretics. These latter, gathering monthly with M. Allar, a sculpture and scholar, are devoted above all to the spiritist magnetism extolled by the late Cahagnet, their true pontiff.

I have seen there a subject named Ravet who converses with the late Cahagnet when the thaumaturge M. Allar puts him to sleep. This M. Ravet is an old man accustomed to these exercises, but what he relates does not go beyond what he hears. They take his hand, and that good, wrinkled face explains to you your future or your past, and recommends to you some small homeopathic remedies. They listen to him respectfully, for, they explain to me, the soul of the late Cahagnet inhabits him at these sacred moments. M. Lecomte de Noisy-le-Roi, naturalist, impregnated with the most subtle spiritualities, questions him on the plants, and M. Allar on metaphysics, - both with conscience and perspicacity.

These students numbering nearly forty, form the most extraordinary assembly: rigorous seekers, mediumistic writers, mystics ill-favored with beautiful, almost savage eyes, adventuring Freemasons, female enthusiasts fallen into neurasthenia, detractors would say, in order to better prognosticate during their sleep the destinies of France; astonished young ladies...

I have been, I must say, overwhelmed with prophetic hopes. If my memory is good (it has been more than two months since I left this learned assembly), there were announced to me troubles in the street, and the growing and brutal rise of socialism during this legislative period... After all, rather clairvoyant oracles.

To be sure, I have emerged from this strange workshop where sits enthroned the statue of Isis, nearly intoxicated by these marvels served up to me by affable laic high priests, appealing to a science a little too permeated with free thought, and chatting with the souls of the dead as easily as one devoted to his confessor, and with no less deference[2].

THE BUDDHISTS

The Buddha counts at Paris more than a hundred thousand friends and at least ten thousand adepts; more especially since they can call themselves Buddhist all while remaining Christian, and since our tenderness for animals and the immense compassion of the moderns for the whole universe seems to us to come from the Orient as an excess of kindness.

Let us look around us: artists, men of letters, frequenters of the boulevards are Buddhists. M. de Esguquiza, brilliant painter, renders worship to Gautama; M. Clémenceau, free thinker, lovingly collects the religious marvels that come to us from Japan; the Baron Harden-Hickey, Saint-Patrice of the *Triboulet*, the senior cries out in many books his impetuous propaganda; M. Kerkof, representative of Volapük at Paris, refused, they tell me, to be an introducer under the peremptory pretext that he was a Buddhist; Germany has coalesced on behalf of those most moved to pity among men, and its most cruelly pessimistic philosophy, that of Schopenhauer and Hartmann, feels the dampness of tears for the suffering of creatures; and there it is which improves humanity at the remembrance of the oriental messiah.

But the Buddhists are far from agreeing with one another. I do not wish to multiply the sects, I will content myself with dividing that philosophical and religious party, in its compact mass, into two camps, that of the crudites and that of the disquieted souls, the official scholars like those of the Guimet Museum, on the one hand, and M. de Rosny on the other.

I
ORTHODOX BUDDHISM

It has been given to me to traverse several times at the Guimet Museum the silent rooms where are heaped up the treasures of India, China, and Japan, in order to commemorate before all Paris the legends of the greatest among men, of the one who, as much as Christ, illuminated Tolstoy, and who triumphs today in the intellectual and curious souls as much, perhaps, as at Benares, more than two thousand years ago.

The reason for this victory of Buddhism in the midst of the blasé intellects of our era, has been discovered by M. Guimet, I believe, in relating to us in his *Promenades Japonaises* what an old priest confessed to him over there: "Buddhism accepts in the other beliefs all that is grand, moral, and good, for the good is always inspired by the sacred heart of Buddha. We often find among the others more truths than we bring thereto, but all that is good emanates from the sacred heart of Buddha," - salutary tolerance which the despotic sects of the Occident always ignore.

I first visited M. de Milloué, the conservator of the Guimet Museum, Rue Mazarine, in his tranquil and laborious house.

"My God," he admitted to me, "I do not believe in the seriousness of the Parisian Buddhists. I believe in the Buddhism which comes to us from the autochthonous lands; in this moment, we have the unhoped for chance to possess among us the most remarkable pontiffs of this religion, M. Horiou-Toki, esoteric Buddhist. You have seen him officiate at the Guimet Museum. How superior he was in gravity and in knowledge to the other two priest who preceded him, from that Sin-Siou sect, that a prince of the imperial family deformed, according to his tastes, by suppressing the abstinence of meat and celibacy! M. Horiou-Toki , who came to us from the Chicago Congress, works for the Guimet Museum at the explanation of the four hundred 'esoteric' gestures, that is to say unexplained for the profane, gestures that he accomplishes during his office under that sort of chasuble which veils him. I do not wish to speak to you but of one alone. Thanks to this invisible gesture, the Buddha descends into his priest. Just as the host, at the words of the Catholic sacrificer, becomes the body of Jesus Christ, at this silent prayer, the Buddhist priest becomes a sort of god; and he may, by his ardent will, allow all the assistants to commune with his divinity. Moreover, the true believers perceive, at this moment, upon the brow of the officiant, five flames of different colors which are his soul delivered..."

"Admirable," I reply, "also, I am no longer astonished at the crowd, with you, of young women."

"It is in great numbers, and with delicious perfumes, that they invade the museum; and, to cite but one to you, I had known Madame Bloch who, having traveled to Tibet, brought us extraordinary anecdotes. Alas! the Buddha soon took her back with him, and she was soon dead to us. As to the scholars, they do not easily tire. You are aware of Eugène and Emile Burnout, Anquetil Duperron, the initiator; M. Chézy, M. Barthélémy my Saint-Hilaire, M. Foucaux, professor at the Collège de France; M. Senart, M. Lamairesse, M. Barth, M. Ferr, and still others. They have devoted, if not their faith, at least their intelligence and their research to this apostle of charity."

M. de Milloué, with his book: *Le Bouddhisme dans le monde*, elucidates the doubts, resolves the confusion, and under our eyes finally wide open, unfolds the adventure of this religion from the depths of its origins to its modern renaissance.

I have been stricken - justly because henceforth they are clearly distinct, at the similar evolution that the faith of Jesus and that of the Buddha have undergone.

Both philosophic and moralist reforms, not of the priest, depended, the one upon the Jewish law, the other upon the Vedic law. They transform, but they continue. If Jesus kept the idea of the one God, it is because he received it from the prophets and from Moses; if Gautama was slightly preoccupied with the innumerable divinities of India, and especially with Brahma, it is because the first Upanishads, the Sankhya, and the Vedas are naturalist, and within their entrails is not contained the germ of a creator God. Neither one innovates; they quite simply conform themselves, the one to the unitary genius of the Occident, the other to the ecstatic genius of the Orient.

For Christ, man is god through filiation to the Celestial Father; for the Buddha, the gods, the real ones, exist only on the condition that they were previously men. They form a sort of invisible Court which rules the affairs of the world, from the heights of their universal detachment.

Thus Jesus said: "It is necessary to be good, because my father is good." Thus the Buddha said: "It is necessary to be good, because to be evil is to be unhappy, it is to remove oneself from the divinity that he must become."

More than arbitrary is life for the apostle of Nirvana; it is not the will of Providence which raises us up or strikes us down, it is our actions in the prior existences which necessitate our unhappiness or our happiness now.

Such is the law of Karma, that the modern spiritists have adopted themselves too.

"A short life, a long life, a state of illness, good health, a bad appearance, a gracious exterior, a lesser power, a great power, poverty, wealth, low birth, high birth, ignorance, knowledge, depend on our conduct in our previous incarnations," says the Cula-Karma-Vibhanga-Suttanta.

And further on:

"The evil actions that you have committed are done neither by your father, nor your mother, nor your relatives, nor your friends, nor your counselors. You alone have committed all of them; you alone are to reap the fruits to yourself."

Will these successions of lives be, therefore, without end? Will not this chain of distress ever end? Yes. But on the condition of permeating oneself well with the four truths taught by the Buddha:

1. Understand sadness;
2. Penetrate its cause, desire;
3. The end of sadness is the love of oneself vanquished, covetousness subdued;
4. Know the path which leads to refuge, to Nirvana.

Karma will no longer construct new dwellings for the one who knows and practices these four truths.

What is Nirvana?

"If someone teaches that Nirvana is to live, tell him that he deceives himself; if someone teaches that Nirvana is to cease being, tell him that he lies; for he does not see the light which shines beyond the broken lamp, he knows not the endless life, the felicity that time no longer measures." (*The Light of Asia* by Edwin Arnold.)

The enormous compassion of Buddha for the world, compassion which the best of men have, depends only upon his horror at sadness In order to flee this sorrow, it is necessary to withdraw oneself from the universe, to remove from oneself all sensations, to hurl oneself into the abyss of nothingness which is Ecstasy. But this flight far from appearance and from the world, has nothing to do with egotism, it is founded in an infinite mercy for all that lives, that is to say suffers - all that suffers is man - and it envelopes in one same love down to the animals and the plants, those inferior sensibilities where sleeps the humanity of tomorrow.

This appeal to a mystical life disengaged from all desire, we find again in the primitive Gospel. Like Jesus, the Buddha also founded confraternities of monks devoted to charity and poverty. By the millions, they followed the ardent apostle, abandoning their goods, cutting their hair.

The women followed this example, but the master admitted them at first with difficulty; he feared them; finally, on the prayer of Ananda, the Saint John of the Ganges, the feminine convents were raised, but with more fierce and persecuting rules. Only no pontiff, no clergy, no ritual.

Alas! Such purity and simplicity did not endure. Just as the first Christian churches, full of devotion and without terrestrial ambition, came to be succeeded by a prideful and conquering sacerdotal hierarchy, the Buddhist congregations formed themselves into a council, drafted precepts, raised temples, instituted no longer the old sacrifices fallen into disuse, but a sort of delicate ceremonial where there were flowers, lights, cakes, and perfumes. The overthrown gods of the Brahmins left upon the new altars a resplendent place for the divinized Buddha, similar to the Brahma himself and to the sun; from then on, the weakening of Buddhism. It is no longer an entirely human religion, so affable and proud of being atheistic, it permeates itself with superstitions, accepts the local divinities, loses its form by all the renascent demons, and overburdens itself with exorcisms and relics. Ah! Its great strength is quickly lost; the old cults having invaded the religion which would destroy them, drive them out; and it migrated into China, Tibet, Japan, and even unto that France which now listens to it and welcomes it.

Are there not very strange connections between Catholicism and Buddhism? Both, at their point of origin, bellicose against the priesthoods, then growing heavy with priesthoods and weakening with temporal power.

To complete the resemblance, we are present today at the creation of a neo-Buddhism parallel to the appearance of the neo-Christianity. M. de Milloué foresees no renewal of warmth and life for humanity. This religion of Nothingness, which counsels the sleep of energy, seems to agree too much with our weakness of soul and our neuroses to be beneficial in the coming age. Schopenhauer and Hartman resuscitated it in order to legitimate the failure of our courage and our intellectual inquiry. M. de Milloué, who knows it well, relates it to us and opens it to us. In reality, Paris and the new world have better things to do than "to grow weak and sluggish at the soporific vapor of oriental narcotics." Far from these perverse mysticisms, faith and knowledge await us, offering to our valor their powerful breasts overflowing with the milk of resurrection[3]…

I I
ECLECTIC BUDDHISM

M. de Milloué spoke to me as a scholar, but I possess a weakness for the apostles; also, I cannot resist my nostalgia of M. de Rosny, that Vogue of Buddhism, who will never be but the mystical deputy of China or Tibet, lands where they do not invalidate him.

I met with him in the old and silent hotel of Duquesne avenue. He resembles a little M. Félix Pyat, with his large beard, his green eyes of revolutionary calm, his indoor jacket of a messianic simplicity. I have suffered his strange prestige in his circular office hallucinated by a Chinese scribe in painted wood. But M. de Rosny is not a magician, this is above all a librarian and a dreamer, the intellectual brother of Tolstoy.

"Ah! So is it written, if you know how many enemies I have, me who preaches universal love. For my part, I do not detest that 'Logomachy' by which men dispute among themselves, having often the same ideas, but not being able to hear each other's words. They have recently denounced me to M. Constans as a corrupter of the youth; and at my course at the Sorbonne (M. Rosny begins to cough), course that I have never been able to inaugurate, my throat being seized, they created for me a heap of difficulties for the entrance cards, for example; for I know that there is much jealousy among the orientalists. They cannot stand, for the most part, that I have some popularity. Renan exercised a true action over the greater public, and they are astonished today that I interest a flock of souls, and that around me are gathered disciples of young men and fashionable ladies."

"They would no doubt like that you limit yourself to remaining a scholar..."

"Scholarship, the texts, are of little import to me; I take my good where I find it, and it matters little to me that so many of my ideas belong less to the Buddha than to Voltaire, Rousseau, or Hegel. I have as much esteem for history as for the gossip of porters. Now, such a system belongs no more to Plato than to Jesus or to Lao-Tzu... We have made such notable progress... The true gospels, for example, reside much more in our memory and in our imagination than in the texts. And it may happen that a cabman knows much more on Buddhism than M. Max Muller, to whom nothing of the Sanskrit is unknown."

"Of that I have no doubt. However, I would desire to understand your Buddhism."

"It is summed up in a phrase: The problem of our destiny, is it foolishness or a subject of anxiety? As to sorting linguistic roots, I consider this work as little important as that of peeling carrots in the kitchen."

"Do you believe in the reincarnation of souls?"

"Absolutely. It is still only an hypothesis, like the law of Darwin, transformism, silly as it is. I do not attempt to explain to you whether we, having been men, are to migrate into the flesh of a beast or into a plant organism. What is certain is that our being is continued: without this, nothing seems logical in the universe."

"An intransigent opinion..."

"I am an intransigent, but, at the example of the Buddha, I do not impose my doctrines. I believe that it is forbidden to convert, I do not teach the truth, I only show the way of the truth. Each must prove within himself his own doctrine. Each must be his own priest. We have, within us, two instruments of knowledge: first the shivers, which brings us into the presence of ideas or beings, and the reason which controls these too personal shivers. When these two instruments are in accord, we have attained the individual truth."

"Have you thought of establishing a Buddhist practice at Paris?"

"They have often proposed it to me, and I imagine that today I would occupy a position other than that of professor at the School of Oriental Languages and at the School of Higher Studies, if I had decided to wear a sacred costume and pronounce some sort of mass upon a new altar. Now, I find it repugnant to play the role of a charlatan, and I adhere to the circular of a Japanese committee which declared: 'To build churches would be to act contrary to the precepts of poverty of the Buddha! Have we not the Christian temples, which are heated and well-lit? It is lawful to us to meditate upon salvation, all while remembering that a pagoda will never be as good as a pure sentiment.' "

Upon the work-table, immense as one found in a workshop - O Tolstoy! - I glimpse papers lying about.

"This is my next book, monsieur," announces M. de Rosny; "my publisher has drawn it from a great number of specimens and has adorned it with a cover in black Moroccan leather, on the request of a multitude of devotees desirous to go to mass with this new missal. Caprice that I dare not criticize, since I am the object thereof as well as my doctrine... Moreover, I claim that the Pope himself is Buddhist...in his fashion..."

I peruse the abstract, and I pause at these suggestive

titles:

> *The Vehicle of Love.*
> *The Cult of Remorse.*
> *The Great Levelling.*
> *The Mercenary Reward.*

"The Vehicle of Love" is the doctrine of the Buddha, that law of egotism abolished and altruism exalted. But are we not all faltering Buddhists? Our relapses are renewed every day. As I was disquieted thereby for myself, the prophet of Duquesne avenue reassured me by asserting to me that it would suffice me to persist in struggling against my vices, despite my little hope of victory. And such is the "Cult of Remorse," which adapts itself to our imperfections. The "Great Levelling" is each in one's place, the woman finally queen at the side of man, king; and as to the "Mercenary Reward," it is our vain desire to do good in order to win a crude heaven or a childish hell, instead of asking before all that the sole Good carry out the good deed, immanent in that Good itself...

When I went back again toward the humid night, M. de Rosny spoke to me of the Woman:

"The regeneration of the woman, her elevation to the rank of strong woman, mother of man, and vestal of the sacred fire of Intuition, is the highest task that is possible to realize in our day in the vast domain of the Great Levelling.

"Here, when women will have taken back the role which is incumbent upon her, and which consists before all in provoking among men the cult of Rectification, of Love, and of Seeking, the law of Becoming shall be established upon its true seat, and the Destiny of beings will be prepared by the surest, most prompt, and most direct path."

This feminist apostle considers writing for his

admirers the *Nouvelle Marguerite* (Gœthe, wake up!) like Rousseau drafted the Nouvell Héloise; and I was still on the staircase when the philosopher related to me this eastern anecdote: "Gautama was wasting his time in caresses with the beautiful Gaupa, when this latter said to him: 'You are going to abandon me, O my husband; how many regrets you will leave me!' The sage responded: 'Calm yourself, my wife; in your next existence you will be reborn a man.' "

Who knows if the future Marguerite will not be the Faust of the future?

It was raining in Paris when I left the admirable and eloquent M. de Rosny. I was melancholic. This amiable religion had not permeated the soul of my coachman, who whipped his horse. I am reminded of the inner distress of the master, regretting not acting much but upon distinguished minds.

"Barely having arrived at Valéry-en-Caux," he admitted to me, "where I was going to stay for the summer, I found a Buddhist coal-man."

In return, I know of noble spirits and delightful hearts which vibrate to the doctrines of Sidhartha, and I soothe myself by thinking of that pious luncheon that I read about in comparison with the Comte Antoine de la Rochefoucauld, the portrayer of the Mayas, of Isis, and of the Angels, which welcomes me with the high priest Horiou-Toki, and where, in perfumes of frankincense and chrysanthemum, we talk only of the divine Nirvana and of the cult of the invisible buddhas.

III

A BUDDHIST CEREMONY

It was a small and melancholic spectacle, that mystery that a superior of the Signon temple, M. Horiou-Toki, declaimed and performed on November 13, 1893, before all of Paris, on the premier stage of the Guimet Museum. The morning light filtered into the room crowded with Buddhas in strange postures set in contemplation; and an astonished meditation permeated the souls of the distracted young women, the aged but attentive gentlemen, and the smiling journalists. All were seated upon improvised benches, to the left and right of a slender priest, enveloped, drowned I dare say, in a sort of pale yellow chasuble, spangled with bouquets of dull flowers. The altar was installed against the immense pedestal where were amassed disparate and luminous idols, an altar slender as him, with, instead of a tabernacle, a miniature pagoda where shone a tiny Buddha. Upon the cloth, eight cups full of white chrysanthemums, an incense burner in the shape of a lotus, two saucers full of rice, a small plate of cake, and a platter of fruits. Two tall red candles with flickering lights, and two large vases overflowing with large flowers crown this discreet repast offered to the gods.

Eight times the thin and yellow hand, like the antenna of a long insect, shakes the small bell, to advise the gods and the men that the grand drama of the union of the priest and divinity is on the verge of completion. Religious entry into the temple: The priest has his fingers joined and he salutes Addi-Buddha, the abstract father of all Buddhas, by this loving invocation: "O! Our Niorai may be compared to nothing; O how marvelously grand he is!" Then this small body, which has the color of tea and of those exciting delights of the Orient leading to dream through intoxication, collapses, nearly disappearing under the sacred cloak. He isolates himself from the whole world in order to better soar up into the beyond which palpitates around him.

Now, everything holds him back yet upon the earth, even these sacred instruments, without doubt too material, and even down to the prayers of the assistants, to disquieted by human covetousness. The consecrated water rests happily in a lacquer-ware cup, and the thin wand that the hierophant soaks therein sits erect at the tip of his fingers, become magical; the drops spread into the air, on the ground, and upon the altar, have purified the entire hall, ready henceforth to welcome the invisible spirits. As to the offerings, already pure; like the fruits of the earth that the hand of man has scarcely grazed, they are exorcized by the *Sango*, a three-pronged staff by which are expelled the lowest demons folded under the petals of the flowers and in the ungraspable interstice which separates two grains of rice.

Now the Buddhas can come, souls of the wise who have already illuminated the earth by their beneficent presence, and the Bodhisattvas, glorious spirits, kinds of guardian angels of the people who may perhaps be incarnated one day into some triumphant apostle. M. Horiou-Toki awakens them and calls them on a tone of recitative chant, infinitely sweet and sad, and neither does he neglect the most humble geniuses, the demi-gods of the hearth, and those devils, good at their core despite their terrible visage, for their mission is to lead the wicked back to the good through terror.

They are all there, in the number of a thousand and sixty-one, visible for the faith of the audience - such are the divinities, even those of India and Japan, accustomed to the passive indifference of men! To thank them, the priest pours out the white chrysanthemums from the six cups and recites: "May these flowers fill the ten worlds and be offered to all the Buddhas and Bodhisattvas!" All this is intermingled with volutes of incense exhaled from a bronze censer whose stem is immobile; triple shakes of the hand-bell, kissed at the moment of being picked up or set down, and whose rhythm recalls the Catholic Sanctus; finally - which makes the longest impression - the gong sounds wrung from a metallic basin to punctuate the mantras or sacred verses.

A sort of papyrus is unfolded by the monk, strange names are proclaimed with the same plaintive accent, that the grave plain-chant of the Carmelites alone surpass in beauty; there are a hundred words, sacred appellations of the gods. But the officiant has just fallen to his knees and, praying for all the assistants and all the beings of the earth and of the stars, he exclaims: "The Buddhas do miracles in the whole universe, and they show themselves therein under multiple transformations according to the circumstances. Nothing can vanquish that eternal strength, capable of fulfilling all prayers."

Three strikes of the bell alert Buddhas and Bodhisattvas that they may withdraw. The priest disappears again under the sacred cloak, cuirass against the innumerable temptations, and he moves away from the altar backwards.

...An anxiety remained with me. M. Horiou-Toki seemed to employ all his wits to veil his hands moving under the pale chasuble. I questioned M. de Milloué, while M. Guimet multiplied here and there his amiability and his commentaries. M. de Milloué answered me: "The officiant takes care to hide from the people during the ceremonies the *mudras*, that is to say the mystical signs of his fingers which, equivalent to the recitation of a mantra or verse, call the celestial energies and converse with them."

Then I am reminded of the old schools of Kabbalists, they too accord a symbolic and effective power to certain words and to certain postures of the face and hands by which the spirits are compelled to obey. In the Occident as in the Orient, one same initiation seems to have presided over the practices of magic. It is true that this science of word and sign, if it has some authority in the invisible, has not much power over the visible, and the English and the Turks, sabre in hand, have always enslaved the learned Kabbalists of Judea or the esoteric Buddhists of India...

Thus, M. Horiou-Toki does not scorn the little advantages that are obtained for him without hieratic pantomime and sacred mutterings, and it is in good Japanese language that he explains to his interpreter, the very Parisian M. Kawamoura, his sharp desire to be sketched by M. Régamey.

The ceremony concluded, I walk around the altar and notice very close to it, a small table where is displayed an earthenware statue of Kooboo-Daishi, founder of the sect to which M. Horiou-Toki belongs. They did not forget to serve a small repast to the effigy of this excellent monk who died around the year 838, but I noticed that the plates were less numerous and all small; for never has a man, had he died in the most fragrant veneration, had the stomach of a thousand and sixty-one Buddhas.

At the base of the altar had fallen the fan and the prayer beads among petals and crumbs.

However, I know not what thrust itself upon my soul, despite the flashy icons of the pedestal, where sneer the benevolent demons with six hands armed with lances and swords, and overlapping green bulls, while behind, in a nimbus, whirls an enormous wheel of torture. I thought of the temples in Japan, the fine architecture adorned with pictures, and statues of a delicate and sumptuous fantasy, in the middle of vast and cheerful gardens, where sparkle, lacquered and gilded, chapels similar to trinkets arranged in tiers a hundred times larger, inhabited by ecstatic and vegetarian monks. Ah! Europe limits Buddhism!... Thus have I explained to myself the disengaged tone with which M. Clémenceau, chance-comer at the end of the ceremony, hat on ears, murmured, while flicking a disgusted finger at the pious offerings:

"Peuh...doll's dinners."[4]

THE THEOSOPHISTS

My mystical youth was traversed by the legend of Blavatsky (H.P.B.), then still living, of that extraordinary Cossack who, in America and Europe, was the head of the Theosophical Society. We have often talked of this on the bank of the sea and in Provence, in the clear mountains where we would be visited by those Angels of light that are the beautiful rays of the sun. She appeared to us at once deadly, beautiful, and wicked, bearing on her brow the dark halo of the Antichrist - destroyer of the gods, tormentor of consciences, and blowing madness into the trumpets of the enormous and magical wisdom of the Orient.

At Paris, I asked around, disquieted by this inauspicious and splendid prodigy. I knew at Montmartre an old man who had formerly approached her, when, very young, she stayed at Paris. He related to me that she was his "subject." In catalepsy, she appeared double: sometimes an archangel spoke through her ambiguous lips, and it was a prodigious and intrepid science; sometimes a demon yelped, hateful and violent. "Thus was she in life," added this magnetizer, "strange, multiple, under a formidable and shabby *influence*; but for all those who knew her, despite her straying and her faults, she remained fascinating."

In *Old Diary Leaves*, M. H. Olcott expatiates upon the faculty that Balvatsky had to yield her personality to superior effluences, be they the spirits of her living and faraway guides, or intelligences not clothed in flesh.

"One summer afternoon, she and I were in our office in New York. Twilight was beginning and the gaslights were not yet lit. She was sitting near the south window, and I was standing behind the chimney and I reflected. I heard her pronounce the following words: 'Look and learn,' and turning my eyes to the side, I perceived a fog which rose from her head and shoulders. Suddenly it took form and resembled one of the Mahatmas. Absorbed in contemplation of the phenomenon, I remained standing and silent. The upper half of the torso alone was visible, then soon disappeared; was it reabsorbed into the body of H.P.B. or not, I do not know. She remained motionless, like a statue, for around three minutes, then she gasped, returning to herself. When I prayed her to explain the phenomenon to me, she refused, saying that it was up to me to develop my intuition in a manner to comprehend the phenomena of the world in which I live... All that she could do was to show me things, leaving to me to make of it what I could..."

... "I remember that, on four different occasions, she gathered in her hand a tuft of her auburn hair, frizzy and wavy, and pulled it out, or cut it with scissors, then held it out to one of us, but then the hairs were found to be coarse, jet black, stiff and absolutely not curly or wavy, hairs which seemed to belong to an Asiatic head and having no relation with those of Madam Blavatsky... An adversary suggested that it was perhaps but a matter of a turn of simple sleight of hand; but my notebook gives evidence that, in one of the cases, the person who received the hairs had had permission to cut them herself with the scissors. I possess two locks taken from her head, both jet black and much coarser than her own; but the one coarser than the other. The one of Egyptian hairs, the other of Hindu hairs. What better explanation has been given of this phenomenon, than to suppose that the men to whom these black locks belonged occupied the mâayâric body of H.P.B., when the hairs were taken from her head?..."

... "I have been tempted to suppose that none of us, her colleagues, have ever known the true and normal H.P.B., but that we have had business with an artificially animated body, a sort of incessant psychic mystery whose *jiva*[5] had been killed at the battle of Montana, where she received five wounds and was gathered up for dead in a ditch..."

... "This woman was successively all ages in one day. The doctor Pike having seen H.P.B. several times, shuddered and said that no one in the world had made such an impression on him. One time he saw in H.P.B. a young girl of sixteen, another time an old woman of a hundred, then again a man with a beard!!..."

... "Furthermore," adds the biographer, "in a very long letter that I received while I was at Bajputana, She is spoken of in the masculine gender and she is strangely confounded with Mahatma M. who was known to be our Guru..."

She returned to Paris, after many excursions among all peoples, and visited madame the Countess of Adhemar and madame the Duchess of Pomar, both Theosophists. She assailed them with marvels; sometimes bells suddenly rung, sometimes flowers spontaneously appeared between her fingers... One day, on a plain, a child on horseback looked back, saw her at his side, speaking of his father and mother who waited for him: finally she added: "Look now right in front of you." The child obeyed... a second later, he could no longer refrain from turning his eyes toward his mysterious comrade. But she had disappeared... On the entire expanse of the plain, there was no Blavatsky.

*

The three hundred Parisians affiliated with the Theosophical Society recognize this intrepid conqueror, today "disincarnate," as the messenger of the human gods of Tibet, the mouthpiece of those secret and faraway governors of the world. Their president, M. Jean Matthews (pseudonym which conceals the novelist A. Matthey, that is to say M. Arthur Arnould), collects himself in the park of Aulnay-sous-Bois, in a solitary villa, where men are scarcely seen, but that the melancholic presence of the Bondy forest haunts.

"One greatly slandered, that madame Blavatsky!" M. Jean Mattheus related to me, to whom I related the attacks of the paper *the Sun*, claiming that she was no thaumaturge, but a charlatan. "What infamy have they not shed upon her! Look, here is her photograph, which argues for her better than my words."

It is her, indeed, eyes dilated, head enveloped in a dark shawl , body packed into a shapeless cloak with, around the waist, a sort of monachal cordelier. Her frizzy hair become thick upon her brow, nearly white. Her eyes are inexplicable, the color of steel, color of those ferocious and divine archangels who, at a glance, devastate the universe. What remains of this woman, in this visage as though crushed by the seal of a terrible will? The nose is flattened, wide like that of all those who strongly love life, the powerful mouth swells a little, in disdain or fury, an enthusiasm, certainly, which could never be gratified here below. Only the hand remains, infinitely aristocratic, so fine, so white, so slender, that they say is from some cherubim from heaven.

At her side sprawls the enormous beard of M.

Olcott, the administrator of this mysterious Society, of which she is the Grand Master.

"Theosophy?" resumes M. Jean Mattheus, "You ask me what it is? What shall I tell you? It has always existed, it is the great esoteric, occult tradition, which began upon the earth even before there were men... It continues and propagates itself through the initiates and adepts. But, at certain periods, it shows itself. Our masters then reveal those of their teachings that they judge best to express. They choose especially the period of the last twenty-five years of each hundred-year cycle. Thus did we see, in the eighteenth century, the appearance of Cagliostro, Saint-Germain, Cazotte, to cite only those latter. Only, I can tell you that this mystical movement, increasing so in our day, must stop on December 31, 1899, in order to resume on January 1, 1975."

"Is Theosophy mixed up with Spiritism and Buddhism?"

"Not in the least. We have no rites of worship and We create no religion, being the universal religion. Certainly, we benefit from the oriental doctrines, and the teachings of the Buddha are related to our own on many points. But we remain persuaded that every philosophical symbol placed at the door of the mass becomes an 'idol,' a coarse fetishism, which the priests end up believing in as the true entities. If we recognize the reality of the phenomena - the spirits, so mocked still, only insult what exists, said Blavatsky - we believe that these manifestations show an altogether inferior order, and that they are above all the feat of mediums possessed by those forces and unaware of their origin, their character, and their aim."

*

M. Jean Mattheus chatted about these transcendences with a wholly patriarchal ease. He appeared to me entirely similar to his portrait, such as the painting and statuary shown to us by madame Delphine de Cool, very gentle, with his flowing jacket, his large inner clothing, his white beard and his long hair, guarding in the back of his blue pupils the youth of immutable truths. Did he tell me all his thoughts on the beyond? I think not. But from his lips was exhaled wisdom as familiarly as in the discourses of Socrates or in the sermons of Buddha.

"Based on this esotericism, ought the Theosophical Society to have, despite the antiquity of its doctrine, some practical projects adapting itself to our contemporary world?"

"Indeed, its three aims are: 1st, to found a universal brotherhood, no longer sentimental, but in some way scientific, for all men are brothers as various accidents of the same substance; 2nd, the study of the sciences, religions, and philosophies of the Far East; 3rd, to create an "esoteric" section, which, under an oath of absolute secrecy, explains to the adepts the meaning of all the symbols and confers to them a power similar to that of the gods of the old cults. We may, through our dreams of such easy marvels, get an idea of this power. But the glory of theosophy is to reserve these secrets for men morally prepared by initiation. If it reigned in the world, the world would be thus preserved by it from deadly chemistry, bombs, that public poisoning that the adulterated produce propagates. The knowledge would be confided only to those good and intelligent."

"Your society, it seems to me, has it not been established in Europe for a long time?"

"It has barely been ten years since we formed a

group in Paris. With Gaboriau and Dramard appeared our first review, the *Lotus*, then the *Revue Théosophique* of madame the Countess of Adhémar, and finally the *Lotus bleu* that I direct with Coulom (Amaravella). Since the death of Blavatsky, madame Annie Besant directs the Society in Europe, M. Judge in America, and M. Keishtley in Asia.

"What dogmas have you professed up to now?"

"First, there has not been any creation."

"We call *manvantara* the incommensurable period of duration of the manifest Universe, not *created* (no creation, in the proper sense of the word, but successions of manifestations) - never having had a beginning and never coming to an end - of the observed Life, of the unique Substance, of the Universal Spirit, different aspects of one sole and same thing, beyond which nothing exists, and to which all periodically returns; and this return, or *night of Brahma*, or *end of the world* in the ordinary erroneous language, we call Pralaya. We are atheists in the sense that we reject the concept of an anthropomorphic God, outside of nature. Thus we do not pray. There is no other God than the unique substance. This substance acts doubly: it differentiates itself and manifests itself in the universe. Such is the movement called *involution* or descent of the spirit into the last kingdoms of matter; then the *evolution* or return of all the beings in to the bosom of that Unique Substance. India calls this the coming and going of things: the day and night of Brahma. The time during which is unfolded this outbreathing and inbreathing of God, we call: the *Manvantara*. The new scientific discoveries verify our belief. Indeed, they nearly admit today that the end of the world will take place by a tightening, a contraction of the All carried along by the inbreathing of an invisible mouth.

"Seven races are to appear upon our planet as seven senses are to manifest in man. We are at the fifth race and the fifth sense. The sense that the mystics call "the third eye," intuition, will be the apanage of the sixth race, which will see the ether, no doubt that radiant state of matter discovered by Crookes.

"It is necessary that each race evolves on seven earths, not on the perceptible planets, but on others that our eyes and our instruments do not grasp. Our globe is but the fourth, and every race is perfected only after the complete course. Then, it re-enters *nirvana*, goal of every soul across the series of reincarnations; nirvana, which is not nothingness, but a state of unlimited happiness which is always perfected, and where our individuality is preserved. Nirvana is a heaven which progresses in a spiral, ceaselessly.

"The same law rules the minerals, the vegetables, and the animals, which, little by little and by passing through all the degrees of the scale, are to become men; but the terrestrial mineral, for example, becomes a vegetable only on another planet.

"The moral consequence of this teaching is that justice reigns in the universe. Remorse is vain. Every action, good or evil, bears within it its fatal consequences. This is why we must act for the good and not egotistically. We shall only penetrate into nirvana entirely with our brethren. As long as the faults of humanity will bind it to reincarnations, we will not be saved entirely. There is such a solidarity between the beings that, if only one of all of us still suffers, all of humanity suffers.

"Whence comes *Karma*, which signifies: 1st, the Law of Causality (we reap what we sow); 2nd, the balance of good and evil for each individual. Karma determines the fortunate or misfortunate experiences of each incarnation."

I rose, preparing to return to Paris, when M. Jean Mattheus detained me again:

"Our visible guide in the end of this century has indeed been Blavatsky; believe me, monsieur, do not listen to the slanderers. This was truly a supernatural woman. She conquered England, America, and Asia. For ten years before her death, she lived as miraculously, condemned by all the physicians. What she said, what she wrote, was often not from her, but came from our invisible masters whom she served. Her power of suggestion was formidable. How many times, at London, she happened to say to someone 'Look at your knees.' And the one who looked perceived, terror-stricken, an enormous spider. Then she would smile: 'That spider never existed, it is I who made you see it. When she was writing *Isis Unveiled* or *The Secret Doctrine*, she sometimes fell asleep from fatigue, for she worked twenty hours each day. In the morning, upon waking, twenty to thirty pages had been written following her own, in different writing, without her knowing how. In India, she failed to die; she was crawling along the path, expiring, when a Mahatma appeared: 'I can save you,' he told her, 'but you must accept all shame, all sorrow, and all scorn.' 'I accept,' she answered. The Mahatma touched her forehead - and she lived. An adept found in Japan the photograph of a group in bronze representing Ko-bo-dai-shi, the founder of the Shingon sect, with two small elementals laying at his sides, awaiting his good pleasure. H.P.B. also has such servants which obeyed her. For my part, I have seen her, elderly, nearly powerless, at Fontain bleu, transform herself abruptly and appear to us perfectly straight, eyes full of light, limbs supple with youth, telling us: 'My masters of Tibet have just sent me their strength with a mystical message.' Ah! monsieur, the fraud had been even more wonderful than the wonder!..."

THE CULT OF THE LIGHT

... When, in the memorable nights of the Sabbat, the black mass is consummated upon the infamous altar among the imprecations and revilements of the host, while upon the moor the dances and drunken kisses subside, and, in grotesque retinue, great toads swollen with venom, with monk's cloaks and hand-bells, their fore-legs supported on thin episcopal croziers, hobbling back to their nests of slime - suddenly with the moon cut by clouds and the enchantments of sorcerers, a pale ray of sunlight follows in a triumphant "cock-a-doodle-doo.' Then the hellish nightmare ravels out like a sickly fume; there is an immense cleaving up in the dawn, then the absolute erasure; and the trampled herbs which straighten up forget all vestiges of the stampings and convulsions... One drop of daylight was sufficient to exterminate Satan and his people; the Light kills the Evil.

Now the sabbats of ages past are reduced to dubious cabals, bourgeois, but always impious, from the little chapels of Bruges to the mysterious headquarters of Paris, here and there, not far from the Pantheon, for example, where, if I listen to the incomplete indiscretions of terrified women, the Pandæmon, invoked by Huysmans, is established; but the sabbat, which has been civilized and adorns itself with science, has always found (if I am to believe a prophetess of Auteuil, madame Lucie Grange) its avenging whip, its condemnation, and its ruin in the *Light*, no longer the light of Men, as formerly, but the light of the Spirits..

I have passed troubling hours on Montmorency

Boulevard, in the parlor of madame Lucie Grange, the windows of which are made hazy from the smoke of the small locomotives passing nearly level. The past year, I visited her after a disconcerting article that she wrote under the title: War on Black Magic! - Oh that I should be deceived into believing that I am entering a magical arsenal! Around me there is nothing war-like: a small stove, a large work table, a pretty parakeet who pirouettes around its bar, two pious pictures representing the Virgin Mary and the Savior, living happily together with masks of Hermes, Apollo, and Isis; finally, hovering over this familiar temple, a large blue standard.

"I sense around me the malevolent fluids of our enemies," madame Grange explains to me tranquilly, "but I do not fear them. I have declared war on the occultists who practice spell-work by the dark path. Any other at this pastime flirts with a danger of death: but Hermes protects me and inspires me... Invisible, often visible, he is always there with me... others too."

At this moment a little noise crackled: it seemed to me that the walls said yes, and that the stove approved with a crackling.

Before my great astonishment the prophetess breaks out in a great laugh: "You see, they answer too... anyone else would turn a deaf ear... but I have learned the language of things, which is often the language of the spirits." "Are they the dead?" I questioned.

"No, not the dead precisely. The majority are too imperfect, too similar to us. Their manifestations are more often inferior. I am in communication with the souls of the souls, with the powers which direct the universe, that you would call the Genii of the Rosicrucians, the Devas of ancient India, the Amschaspands of Persia, the Sephiroth of the Kabbalah, the Cherubs of Chaldea, or the Archangels of the Apocalypse. One of them has attached itself to me. At first he told me to call him Salem, an Egyptian priest, then he revealed to me that he was Hermes himself, the great Hermes, decided to serve the poor and ignorant woman that I am in order to renew the universe."

I opened my eyes wide and perceived, not without some surprise, that my interlocuter was perfectly sincere in speaking to me in this way, and that I nevertheless have no business with a madwoman. This calm visage, with dilated and changing pupils, that mouth marked by the fold of a smile that does not grow smaller, that modest attire, this easy elocution of a slightly monotone harmony, all envelopes me with a sort of indefinite charm, not irritating, rather sweet, almost lenitive...

"Be astonished no more, monsieur," she continued, "you are here in the modern Memphis. We receive here visits from the greatest men of all times."

"But how do these supra-terrestrial beings enter into communication with you?" "After several days of rapture, I spend an entire night speaking or writing. I am seeing in the conscious state, without being put to sleep by anyone. It is in this way that I have obtained the fluidic resurrection of an Egyptian papyrus. Salem-Hermes comes to me: sometimes he causes to pass before my eyes pictures and symbolic images, sometimes he brings us other intelligences, like those of Marcellus, Miriam, Saint Michael, who reveal to me resplendent truths."

"So Lucie Grange and the prophet Daniel are close relatives," I exclaim. "

Lucie Grange?... I don't know. There is within me

an entirely changed soul which shows itself in these ecstasies, and against which my usual personality sometimes revolts. I do not know only Lucie Grange, I know the medium *Hab...*, diminutive of *Habimelah*, which means, according to the commentary of Hermes, 'Strength of the Father.' "

This Auteuil apartment distorted according to my excited imagination by these admissions whose tone truly far surpasses that of ordinary conversation. And, looking into the past, I thought of the tripod of Endor, the lair of Tryphonius, those fumes of Alecton which cause delirium in the hysterical Pythia. Ah! To think that the train station next door, symbol of contemporary materialism, could not prevent the old oracles from being reborn! Ah! We begin all anew!...

"Hab," insists madame Lucie Grange, "reads into 'the Light.' "

And I whispered to myself: "Yes, it is that, the Light, the ancient cult of the Light, the worship of Ormazd by Zoroaster, the survival of the old time magic reappearing in a faraway corner of Paris, despite the disparagement of the previous sages, - headstrong cult of the great invisible river which, according to the Kabbalists, bathes the world; imagination of God where the spirits, the souls of the dead, the angels and the demons roll in waves..."

Does the priestess of the Light doubt my reflections! She resumes:

"If I have declared war on black magic, it is pushed by my guides from the beyond, by Hermes. I have presentiments of terrible struggles..."

I shake off, while leaving, the atmosphere of the miracle, and it is only several months later that I am reminded of this strange conversation; we had gotten mixed up, my friends and I, with torrid and mystical adventures. There were the dead and madmen in the tragedies of modern occultism... Do we know what is true, what is false? What master gave us the ability to distinguish the truth infallibly?

These days I have penetrated again into the "Pyramid" of Auteuil.

The blue flag flowed with a sort of magnanimous ostentation.

Madame Grange advanced, more serene than usual, and with tranquility:

"You see, the Light has conquered, I think no more of black magic. It is forever overthrown. We are here some friends who gather together with the peace and gaiety of the first Christians."

At this moment, someone entered.

"M. Christian Jr., called the medium Hab."

The visitor bowed with grace, then sat, and I saw him peruse parchments with odd signs, as well as some archeological boards.

The anecdotes resumed. Hab related to me the recent invasion with her of the evil spirits under the form of wasps. "They rushed down toward me," she told me, "I believed that they were going to devour me. But Hermes was there. The wasps were driven back, and their troop, hurling themselves at the window, fell dead. We scraped up no more than small, black creatures, dried up and burnt." The anarchy was not omitted, as fitting, and Hab edified me by narrating how she had formerly, through her sole presence, saved one of his relatives from an attack by the gang at Ravachol; but what appeared most remarkable to me is a feat of sight which would deserve to become historical - history being nearly always fabulous. "One evening," asserted madame Grange, "I saw Bismark performing black magic; he killed and tormented men at a distance; I was shocked, but Hermes told me: 'You will see, he will be punished...' A short time later, I saw him again in the German campaign, surprised by the vintagers who, not having recognized him, amused themselves, according to their custom in this season of merry-making, by crushing grapes over his figure, putting baskets on his head, and dressing him with vestments of derision."

The grimoire peruser rose:

"Monsieur," he said to me, "I am an archeologist, and I confess to being quite disconcerted by the phenomena which have occurred in this house. I must, however, recognize the reality thereof. Flowers and branches fall from the ceiling upon the heads of the experimenters during the séances. Very heavy objects are displaced. Recently, madame Grange believed to have seen Napoleon; he announced to her that he would soon manifest. Indeed, the next day, at the said hour, we were jostled about by a terrible wind which crossed the staircase and we thought to be overturned..."

"No, no," I exclaimed, "that is to become insane!"

M. Christian Jr. gazed at me with his very fine blue eye under long eyelashes. At first, he evoked rather well that red man who appeared to the sorcerers when they had sacrificed the traditional black hen...

Having taken some steps toward me, and after having consulted a little compass, he grasped my hands with effusion.

"I congratulate you, monsieur, you have just seated

yourself between the East and the North. These are the most fortunate points, and the one who spontaneously places himself in this corner cannot be a wicked man. If you had set yourself in the South you would be a false friend, in the East a miser, in the West a slanderer, in the North a hypocrite and envious. Such are the mysteries of the Holy Kabbalah and the best manner to be enlightened on one's relations..."

I took my leave a few minutes later, very pensive and persuaded that Marie Alacoque had been reincarnated, and persuaded that perhaps the "Red Man of the Tuileries" was not a fable.

VINTRAS, BOULLAN, AND SATANISM

It has been given to me to be mixed up in the tragic adventures of the dying Vintrasism. With scarcely anyone sharing the doctrine of Stratanael (Pierre-Michel Vintras), reincarnation of the prophet Elijah, the circumstances have required me to defend - even on the field of combat - as in the times of religious quarrels, his successor, the friend of J. -K. Huysmans, the Abbé Boullan, the most extraordinary thaumaturge of our positive century, Grand Pontiff of the Carmel, calling himself the very soul of John the Baptist - in short, the doctor Johannes of *Là-Bas*.

I do not lament these little derangements, for I am recognizing in Vintrasism intellectual surprises that this little known cult has bestowed on me, feast of the most blasé curiosities.

*

In 1839, on August 6, at Tilly-sur-Seules, Saint Michael the archangel revealed his mission to the foreman of a paper factory, named Vintras, and informed him that Elijah had descended into his soul in order to prepare the coming of the Paraclete. This ecstasy transformed this modest and pious worker, to whom it communicated a lyricism unknown since Ezekiel; this was the starting point of a turbid and brilliant odyssey, intersected with angelic conversations, battles against black magicians, excommunicatory briefs, bewildering wonders, and a little prison.

Whoever knew and approached Vintras submitted to the charm of his word and his imperious majesty. Like the shoe-maker Jacob Bœhme, he received at one single time the knowledge of all things sacred without having read anything and knowing almost no scripture. Princes, priests, monks, and nuns were won over by the prestige of this mysterious spirit.

He radiated over Paris - where he still counts today numerous adepts - from the Carmel of Montplaisir, a suburb of Lyon. There was his temple with, under his orders, the two priests, M. Soidekerck, old maker of chasubles, and the Duc de Parme.

J. -K. Huysmans knew, two years ago, Soidekerck, an old man a little worn out by the practices of the mysteries, who confided to him plaintively: "Ah! Monsieur, my master made me write all night."

"And who, then, is your master?" asked the writer of *À Rebours*.

"God, monsieur, God," replied the pontiff.

It is at Montplaisir that the pilgrims still find the altar of Vintras, surmounted by a "hostiary   cross,"   the wheat of which, spangled with strange bloody geometries, begins to be tormented a little by disrespectful worms. In the very time of the prophet, he celebrated there, in a chamber hung in red, the provincial sacrifice of Mary, a sort of mass in French in honor of the Holy Virgin: the hosts themselves emerged from the chalice, where a real blood flowed from the ceiling and, in his prayers, the thaumaturge, surpassing the wonders of the medium Eusapia, recognized as scientific today, rose from the ground as if made to ascend by the invisible hands of the Angels.

Stranger scenes still unfolded here. The prophet, supported on his altar, combatted the black masses that he claimed to see at a distance at the moment when they were said at London and Rome by prelates and political men in league against the Carmel.

The Carmel, indeed, had allied itself with Naundorff and claimed, by mystical ways, to conduct to their throne those evicted, yet rather dangerous candidates, in order to be condemned by the courts of Europe and the Sovereign Pontiff.

Vintras was becoming cumbersome. They profited by some famous defections, like that of Gozzoli, to accuse the Carmel of being a receptable of impurity, and they arrested the thaumaturge, suspected of having extorted sums from his faithful.

The ladies Cassini and Garnier, one of whom gave him 800 francs, and the other 3,000 francs, admitted to the tribunal that these presents were voluntary. They condemned the prophet none-the-less, to a 1,000 franc fine and five years confinement. Vintras lowered his head; but in other respects, his was a vain imprisonment. Having the gift of bilocation, he appeared ceaselessly to his friends and pontificated all the same at the Carmel, while his body alone remained shut up at Rennes.

Note that in the search of his house, "God took it upon himself," according to a disciple, "to conceal all that he did not wish to allow to be seized... What would these gentlemen of the court say if they learned what their eyes have not seen, what their hands have not sensed, very precious objects to be discovered, and upon which their gaze and their hands have been turned ten times?"

Events took it upon themselves to avenge Vintras. Bardout, who refused to plead for the prophet for fear of ridicule, became mad shortly after. Mgr. Paysant, bishop of Angers, died after a dinner where he attacked Pierre-Michel; Mgr. Varin, bishop of Strasbourg, having written an article against the Carmel, suddenly perished...

Yet the doctrine of Vintras did not deserve such fulminations. It limited itself to these three points:

1.   Immaculate conception of the Virgin Mary (not yet recognized then by the Holy See).

2.   Angelity of our souls before terrestrial life.

3.   Hell is not eternal (Vintras called his church the "Work of Mercy").

*

The Abbé Boullan, doctor in theology, long time director of the *Annales de la Sainteté*, only mystical Catholic review of these latter years, then shut up in the dungeons of the Inquisition at Rome, for having, he said, healed a possessed person with the seamless robe of the Savior, adopted these dogmas, and, having become John the Baptist, succeeded Vintras-Elijah.

He was not recognized by all the Vintrasists of Paris and Lyon. The first divided themselves into two chapels, the one at Montrogue, the other in the environs of the Rue Sainte-Anne, under the direction of the wife of an old banker. The second gathered themselves around a carpenter.

M. Leymarie, the representative of the Kardecist spiritists, has related to me, if my memory is good, that he saw Vintras officiate, at Paris, with a gendarme. Dr. Martin, descendant of the famous Martin de Galardon, still continues, near Luxembourg, the cult of the "Prophet."

The Abbé Boullan was a very small man with powerful jaws, with illuminated eyes, with a good smile, and a gentle and simple heart. I found him, at Paris and Lyon, very different from his predecessor, who, a giant with a very long head, displayed an immense fan-shaped beard. Both bore strange mystical signs on the face drawn by the wrinkles. Vintras had a dove clearly traced out between his eyebrows; and Boullan showed, at the corner of his left eye, the Kabbalistic pentagram (the five-pointed star), very visible in the latter days of his life.

M. J. -K. Huysmans and I have visited the modest sanctuary of the Rue La Martinière at Lyon. The astral battles were indulged in there, frightening and a little chimerical, having as its field of battle the small altar where Boullan celebrated, barefoot, the sacrifice of glory and of Melchisekek, by which would be stricken down the canon Docre de Bruges, the black magicians of Paris, and the great operators of Rome... In fact, M. J. -K. Huysmans has related to me, and I have been able to verify these facts, that he relieved souls tormented by Satanism, healed the possessed and even animals, cleared away as with a wave of the hand stomach distensions, and, with the help of candles and salt, prevented the breaking of tissues.

The "spell-casters" avenged themselves by never leaving him tranquil. He showed me his thumb permeated to the bone by Satanic effluvia, and fluidic pistol balls hollowed out even more his ascetic chest.

The painter Lauzet, passing through Lyon, verified one evening the rumor of invisible fist blows upon the forehead of the officiating pontiff. His forehead was swollen with bumps and he fainted, for he was left surprised, having begun the fight too late.

Like J. -K. Huysmans, I have preserved the most stunning memory of this "Waterloo in the void."

This small man, warned by the flight of the sparrow-hawks, seconded by the excellent seer, madame Thibault, who, eyes raised above her spectacles, perceived the legions of the angels and demons - the host, like a sword in the fist, bounded, invoking the Glaivataires and the Invincibles, entirely enveloped by a long robe of vermillion cashmere, fastened at the waist with a red and white cordeliere, with, above, a cloak cut over the chest in the shape of a cross, head lowered.

This warrior of the invisible was after all the most gentle of men. He too shared that sort of malediction that weighed upon Vintrasism. He was condemned by a tribunal of the Empire on this sole grounds: "Given that the Abbé Boullan could not have had any conversation with the Virgin..." "But it is just that he should be able to prove it," M. J. -K. Huysmans told me, who refuses, not inappropriately, the magistrature the right to deny the miracle in principle. As to the theory of doctor Johannes on the "unions of life," it was, I believe, misinterpreted in a profane sense, this term designating only those mystical marriages of which Therese, Marie d'Agréda, and Solomon ceaselessly speak.

He died in his dream, convinced that he would see the Archangel of the Apocalypse opening the heavens with his trumpet in order to cry out: "There is no more time." Believing to announce the glorious kingdom of Jesus for the era of the Paraclete, he remains for impartial intellects the last of the millenarians and exorcists, and a manner of dark martyr, where there were too many illuminated.

M. Rau du Fort at Champigny then became the Grand Pontiff of the Carmel, but not for long. His wife found him one day, lying across his bed, dressed, and dead... It is she who now celebrated the mass of the glory of Melchizedek all alone, under the species of red wine, the male priests alone officiating with white wine.

Poor Vintrasism! Ceaselessly trod down, it still palpitates, here and there, but dispersed and melancholic, consumed by its miracles, defamed by its heresies[6].

THE CULT OF HUMANITY

Who could have foreseen, when Auguste Comte, hoisting his motto: "Without God or King," threw himself into atheistic predications, that he would go on, even him, to consider himself a redeemer and that he would found a religion[7]?

Questioned on this observation by a reporter who had read the *Catéchisme positiviste*, M. Zola commented on this transformation in an ironic phrase: "Me too," he said, "I would perhaps be given to these oddities when I am old and my brain is less lucid."

Indeed, Littré and madame Comte claimed that the most scholarly of the philosophers did not have his full reason when he wrote his testament and deified his wife; but the tribunals did not adopt, any more than the best disciples, any less respectful opinion.

However, it seems to me that if Auguste Comte had incontestably kept a very serene intelligence, his heart submitted to those tempests which inexorably strike the mature man. He was in love.

All lovers undergo a religious crisis. Madame Clotilde de Vaux performed, in the main, but an easy miracle with her beautiful pure eyes scourged by life, her literature of a scholarly woman, and that precaution, so touching, that she took to die quickly, so as not ever to be forgotten...[8]

*

I know that a Chilean, M. Lagarrigue, continued at Paris the cult of Auguste Comte. Rightly, on this point, he had a bone to pick with that excellent M. Laffitte who has too much or too little skepticism to accept a pontificate, and who contents himself, teaching at the College of France, to propagate the scientific doctrines of the master. M. Lagarrigue is an apostle. I saw him on the first floor of 155 Rue Saint-Jacques, small, smiling, but with eyes so keen and a Spanish eloquence, in that conference hall which awaits, I think, only the assessments in order to become a sanctuary. If he has not persuaded me, he has charmed me.

"The Virgin Mother," he told me, "a utopia of Auguste Comte, an ideal, a limit. Our initiator believed that one day the baseness of love would be abolished; that, in order to become mother, the woman would dispense with man; that her thought would suffice to fertilize that human egg that she bore within her..."

I lift my eyes, and, beyond the lined-up chairs, I notice a photograph of the "Virgin and Child" by Raphael... Yes, there indeed is the goddess; on the frame, in large letters, this word: HUMANITY.

Below are the portraits of Clotilde de Vaux and Auguste Comte. She opens wide eyes of the Virgin scorned by life; the pure oval of her face is caressed by her long hair which flows over her cheeks; a sort of school-satchel that she opens up, she reads the letters from her lover, to whom she revealed, far from any impurity, that there is something beyond knowledge, and that this something is Love.

"How beautiful she is!" I tell M. Lagarrigue, who answered while smiling: "She had, however, the custom of saying: 'I have no beauty, I only have expression.'"

The chaste bosom of the lover is veiled by the letters of the prophet whose clerical and authoritarian look reminds me of the aqua fortis of Baudelaire by Manet. It is the same lips made tight by the systematic spirit, nearly identical eyes such as they are opened unmercifully clear upon life; the forehead is that of the popes, wide and high, the collar has the feel of the cleric and the professor, but the ensemble breathes a free-flowingness, more discreet than with the poet of the *Fleurs du Mal.*

Upon a platform, a table and an arm-chair, dominated by the bust of the master, with, below: *Family, Country, Humanity.*

The only frames hung on the side walls contain the images of Charlemagne and Descartes, two positivist saints.

"The rites? The prayer?" continued M. Lagarrigue, "the exaltation of our most beautiful faculties, thanks to the remembrance of the dead. I, for example, who has no wife, pray each day to my mother, and it is her existence in my heart which becomes my talisman against the trials. Subjective life, alas! for we do not believe in the immortality of the soul but through the memory that we have kept thereof. The chastity counseled by Auguste Comte goes so far as eternal widowhood when one of the two spouses dies before the other, a charming and delicate custom which truly divinizes the one who has departed! Thus, our dead, who do not, as for the Catholics, have a survival in a beyond, govern better the living by the marvel of nothingness and the tomb..."

Auguste Comte wrote: "Whereas our old God could not accept our homages without weakening himself by a puerile vanity, the New (the Great-Being, the ensemble of the dead) accepts nothing but our earned praises, which betters him as well as us."

Providence wears four forms: she is material with the "patriciate" (wealth, industry); general with the "proletariate"; moral with the women, spontaneous priestesses of humanity, educators of man until the age of fourteen; intellectual with the male priesthood to whom is reserved, in case of dissention, the pacification among the proletariate and the patriciate.

*

10, Rue Monsieur-le-Prince, where lived Auguste Comte, where Clotilde de Vaux often descended, where the last mystics of positivism flow in pilgrimage[9], I have found only a library, a small room crowded with issues of "la Revue Occidentale," the organ of the group; at the back, a kitchen; other rooms still that I do not see.

They refer me to Rue d'Assas: "M. Laffitte is certainly there."

Upon seeing M. Laffitte, I was stricken to find at last a matter-of-fact man. His large figure, where beard and white hair suppose a veneration, had no pact with mysticism. I sense that he scorns me with the most amiable good grace. First as journalist, for I address a large public, the multitude of which - these are his own words - have no need for a man who meditates; then, these religious preoccupations seem to him entirely useless. "But these are misinterpreted words... Auguste Comte spoke of the sentiments in a scientific language. Clotilde de Vaux was a personal affection, similar to the affection of d'Alembert for mademoiselle de Lespinasse. Nothing mystical in their letters... The cult of the woman?... Certainly, the woman is extraordinary since she gives birth to us." - "Indeed," I say, "and she inspires us..." - "Not always; had Archimedes need of a muse? Moreover, my mother was an atheist from the age of twelve, and I recall that she greatly shocked Monseigneur Dupanloup in speaking of the 'provisional services of God.' Postivism is a religion only in the sense of tying all men together through science. We want to replace revelation with demonstration, and to create an uninterrupted chain from arithmetic to morality. By Jove! We are not the enemies of Catholicism, we recognize its former services, and sometimes we even wish it were more powerful to defend the traditions that we love. It has allowed itself to be beaten on the question of divorce, whereas our will is joined with their own for the triumph of the durable union. I go so far as to regard Ignatius as one of the greatest types of humanity, and I am concluding a study on the Jesuits[10] where Catholics may recognize only my impartiality. If I were not a positivist, I would be Catholic... We have no more principles; the anarchy of our day is above all intellectual. All evil comes from this..."

"... 'Love, order, and progress,' such was the motto of Auguste Comte; what a devil! Progress can exist only through the development of order... without this, mistrust progress..."

*

The learned M. Laffitte then knocked down Hugo and Napoleon (he calls this latter the "sucker of Sainte-Hélèn"), and as he was asserting to me that the fetishism of Comte was similar to that of the poets, who fabulously and through metaphor accords life to objects and things, I owe it to myself, in perusing the "Testament" and the "Catéchisme" of the master, to study this profoundly religious concept, which goes so far as to erect a temple to Humanity.

Let us first consider the role of women - I was going to say the cult - according to the atheistic prophet.

Reason and activity appertain to man, sentiment to the woman. To the woman, as to the people, positivism opens up a noble social career at the same time as just personal satisfactions. This sex is certainly superior to our own as concerns the tendency to have sociability prevail over the personality. This is the purest type of humanity, that no emblem could worthily represent under the masculine form. Its superiority is immediate as to the real aim of all existence; but its inferiority is revealed as to the various means to attain the goal. Every kind of force for the body and for the mind - goes back to man. The practical life being dominated by force, not by affection, women must modify by affection the spontaneous reign of force.

Public life appertains to men, and the existence of women is essentially domestic.

There is a fundamental similarity between the social condition of women and the condition of the philosophers and scholars.

The empire of the real world belongs even less to the thinking beings than to the loving beings, though doctoral pride be less resigned than feminine vanity. The intellectual force is not more moral than the material force. Both constitute means, the morality of which depends on their use. Love alone is directly moral because sociability must prevail over personality. All practical supremacy belongs to activity (the people).

At first purely affective, the moderating force (that of the woman) then becomes rational when the mind rallies to it. It remains to it only to become active by the spontaneous accession of the popular masses.

Force emanates from number and wealth.

Women are the spontaneous priestesses of Humanity[11].

Three cults.

First the private cult which demands three daily

prayers: at sunrise, before sleep, and in the middle of the day. In his "Testament," Auguste has left us his own; but each invents them and performs them according to one's individuality. The morning prayer lasted for him from 5:30 to 6:30, with "commemoration" and "effusion," sometimes standing, sometimes kneeling before the altar. The altar was the red chair where sat Clotilde de Vaux on her visits to the philosopher. Her evoked image then appeared to him as the very image of Humanity. Ordinarily it was veiled, this chair, with a green cloth, lifted only at the most important ceremonies, and the pontifical lover was seated there only when he performed the sacerdotal function. Touching ceremonies! The most serious and most austere of men venerating the flowers and the relics of the departed, and exciting themselves by them unto approaching God; and it ended thus: "To my noble patroness, as personifying Humanity: *Virgine Madre, figlia del tuo figlio, amor te plus quam me, nee me nisi propter te.* (Virgin Mother, daughter of your son, may I love you more than myself, and may I love myself only for you.)" In the evening recommenced sometimes sitting up, sometimes lying down - the commemoration and the effusion, intersected with verses from Petrarch and ending with this cry: "*Addio, Clotilde! Addio, Lucia! Addio, quella che emparadisa la mia mente, Addio!*" The prayer in the middle of the day, around 10:30, shorter than the previous one, lasted only ten minutes, and Dante and Virgil doing the most over-all.

*

The domestic cult embraces nine sacraments: 1st, *the presentation*, a sort of baptism where the child is offered to the Goddess; 2nd, *the initiation*, where the child passes from the arms of its mother to the school of the priests; 3rd, *the admission*, by which the adept of twenty-one years engages himself to serve Humanity; 4th, *the destination*, which around the age of twenty-eight consecrates the social function; 5th, *marriage*; 6th, *maturity*: the man of forty-two learns the inflexible responsibility which begins for him; 7th, *the retreat* given at sixty-three years, which marks for the elder the free choice of successor; 8th, *the transformation*: at the approach of death, the priesthood mingles the regrets of society with the tears of family; 9th, *the incorporation into the Great Being* which presides, seven years after the funeral ceremonies, over the stately transfer of the sanctified remains of the just into the sacred Woods which surround the temple of Humanity.

This Temple of Humanity, where the public cult is to be carried out, is a temple to Death, more real than Life, worthy of being realized by spirits: cemetery, school, curacy, amphitheater, library, sanctuary - a sort of intellectual city and necropolis. Let us note, to be brief, that the side chapels are dedicated to the thirty great types of the positivist calendar, save the last, the most agreeable of the choir, attributed to Heloise, holy among holy women. The feminine statue of Humanity - recalling without doubt Clotilde de Vaux - dominates the terminal area.

And it is thus that this positivist, the most idealist of lovers, rewarded a young woman for having smiled at his white hair.

THE LUCIFERIANS

La Semaine religieuse de Paris, official organ of Catholicism, has recognized the existence of the Antipope Lemmi, to whom the Palladists, last September 20th, confided the tiara of Lucifer. The cult of the Antichrist is now a fact, and the Church no longer ignores it. Already, Fr. Deschamps, M. Claudio Saunet, Mgr. Fava, Dom Benoit, Mgr. Meurin, M. the Abbé Mustel of Coutances divulged many times the modern progress of the new Devil, announced by the Apocalypse and whose reign shall begin in the twentieth century, according to the prophets.

Here are the extraordinary documents that I hold from the doctor Bataille, initiated into the cult of Lucifer, but who did not ever cease being Catholic and practicing, even during his passage into the sect:

"Under the Masonry which is at the point of death, unconscious, a formidable religion has sprung up, Palladism, which has its Supreme Directory at Charleston, the Jerusalem of the Messiah of hell, its executive committee at Rome, and its administration at Berlin.

"In order to become a Palladian, it is necessary to be affiliated with the rite of Misraim and of Memphis, to bear the title of Knight Kadosh, and, in every case, not to be a thirty-third degree with the ring, like M. Floquet, for once one has received the ring, one is incapable of any mystical initiation. The aim of Palladism is not the simple conquest of political power, but the possession of the entire world and its de-Christianization. Here are recruited the Grand Inspectors General on permanent mission, "proofs of friendship," such as Cornelius Herz, Hœnkel,

Bleichrœder. Among them, two women: Mlle. Sophia Walder and Mlle. Diana Woghan.

"They have spoken much on the two Luciferian priestesses, and M. François de Nion recounts the blaze, upon the bare shoulder of Sophia, of the prophecies against the Holy See. In the grand evocatory séances, this virgin serves as prophetess; her revelations were proof of it. But what gives to the one called also 'Sapho' these terrible powers (one of which is 'bilocation') is that she was designated by Lucifer in person to become the great-great-grandmother of the Antichrist. 'The number of popes of Adonai and Jesus is limited,' she will confess to you; 'I will be a mother at the age of thirty-three of a daughter who herself, at the age of thirty-three, will set upon the world another daughter, and the last of the stock will be the mother of the Antichrist; this latter, existing now in the state of demon, inclines himself already toward me when, with Chambers and Mackey, we call him; and he calls me Holy Mother.'"

Monsieur the Abbé Mustel, from the clergy of Coutances, editor at the *Revue Catholique* of this diocese, having spoken repeatedly on the cult rendered to the devil by this strange sectarian that several call the woman with the serpent, received from her this significant letter:

(Here is the Palladian Triangle)
New Reformed Palladium
Sovereign Grand Mastership
of
France, Switzerland, Belgium
under the immediate obedience
of the
Dogmatic Supreme Directory of Charleston.

In the Central Valley
under the eye of D∴ L∴ (Deus Lucifer)
and in the bosom of our
Holy Mother Lodge of Lotus
Orient of Paris
February 2, 000893

"Monsieur,

"One of our sisters of Cherbourg makes known to us that a short-robed Jesuit, acting evidently according to your instructions and spying for your benefit, submits to an inquiry on the subject of a question of order entirely private. Our duty is to make you see that we do not occupy ourselves with what occurs in your convents. Consequently, please give counter-orders to your informants; otherwise they may well smart for it, we warn you well thereof. Involve yourselves with saying your mass. We, ourselves, say our own as it suits us. Each honors the divinity as he understands it.

"Therefore, cease occupying yourselves with what does not concern you.

"Sophia."

"Palladism makes use of carbonarism and anarchy in order to destroy the present society and to build upon its ruins the cult of the one that it calls 'the good God.' It has its pope (the first was Albert Pike), its holy city, Charleston, its Vatican, and its Most Serene Grand Council of Cardinals, to whom Lucifer ritually appears. It is even one of its customs to scoff at our Adonai: 'Look,' it says, 'at the impotent one! His pope cannot even make him appear; he is vanquished and already dead upon this earth as on the other stars - from where I have driven him, my Lucifer!'

"At Paris, where they do not yet have at their command a great power, the Luciferians possess two temples: the first on Rue Rochechouart, not very far from the Sacred Heart; the second on the left bank, quite near the archbishop. One of them is the famous Saint-Jacques triangle. They say the 'white mass' there, and Masonic meetings with evocations take place there.

"On Friday, at three o'clock, Lucifer shows himself at Charleston, and he also manifests in the various centers, save at Rome.

"The 'white mass' is the mass turned around. The 'Elect Mage' or the 'Templar Mistress' who pronounces it wears a chasuble with the cross upside-down. The communion is given under the two species; the host is black with the real presence of Lucifer. And the officiant begins thus:

"*Introiba ad altare Dei optimi maximi.*"

"Upon the retable of the altar, Lucifer, young man with wings deployed, seems to descend from heaven in flames. His right hand exalts a torch, his left pours out a horn of plenty. He tramples a crocodile - papacy and royalty - wearing the tiara and the crown. Below the idol, on the table of the altar, three statuettes: the first, Beelzebuth, with the terrestrial sphere entwined with a serpent near him, raises his hand to announce the arrival of Lucifer; the second, Astaroth with a gentle visage, with two fingers adorned with a rose, holds against her thumb the medal of the Bull; the third, more terrible, Moloch, grips an axe and defends himself with a sort of shield where is sculpted a lion's head...

"The Gospel of the mass is extracted from the

book Apadno, written in green ink by Lucifer and signed by him. This manuscript, given to Albert Pike, is kept secret in the *Sanctum Regnum*, in the triangular altar of Charleston, where no longer is displayed the idol of Lucifer, but God himself, the Baphomet that no human force may wrest from his temple. It resembles the Androgynous Goat of the Templars, but the caduceus has been replaced by the rose upon the cross, at the foot of which the Pelican sacrifices itself."

To comment upon these strange revelations would be to weaken them. Certainly the weariness of our age was necessary to imagine or to re-establish this religion of the fallen Archangel. Ought I add that the Luciferians despise the Satanists and see them like so many contemporary occultists? Their morals endeavor to be as pure as our own, for it is not the God of evil that they worship, it is the "Good God," and they call Adonai "the Wicked God." The doctor Bataille has also asserted to me that they already possess India and China, that America is going to be conquered, and into Europe is going to be delivered the supreme and definitive battle.

Assuredly, if these societies of thaumaturges were not formidable adversaries (an immense schism would prepare itself in the Catholic Church) - it would be necessary to praise them for dazzling us with such a pompous display of miracles; the fairy-scenes do not amuse but children; but things too scintillating are sometimes deceitful, and I greatly fear that these temples, these priestesses, these angels, and these gods are more often naught but the hallucinations of a flame-dream.

ESSENISM

I went to Rue des Belles-Feuilles to chat with madame Marie Gerard, delegate of the Essene groups.

It was barely two years ago that I learned of the survival of this very ancient sect, on which Renan himself could not have been perfectly informed. If I am to believe the Visions of the Blessed Catherine Emmerich, Jesus, as a young man, delighted in strolls and chats with them. M. Edouard Schuré, the Christian initiate, comes to agree scientifically with the inspired. Christ, such as he conceives him, went through the degrees of initiation of these therapeuts who, like him, possessed the secrets of healing and the gift of resuscitation.

I have found the Grand Essene of Paris in a small hall, in front of its library, dressed somberly, with the headstrong visage of an apostle and austere eyes which seek to persuade.

"Our cult is the most beautiful and the most pure," madame Gerard related to me, "for it has never persecuted, it has always been trodden down and it has suffered ceaselessly!"

"At least it still exists. I believed it had, since the death of the Savior, disappeared from history."

"But, monsieur, it has been perpetuated traditionally, and it is thanks to its energy that France has been able to remain a great nation. Joan of Arc was an Essene; she was the second Messiah, the feminine Messiah who had to complete the work of the male Redeemer. This so-called sorceress was but an Essene; we lay claim to her entirely."

"Your dogmas are differentiated, then, from the Catholics?"

"Certainly! We love Jesus, but we hate Saint Paul, who was neither spiritist nor feminist. Moreover, here is our profession of faith:

"1. We worship the Eternal Absolute Just God, as father and mother of humanity.

"2. Our two Messiahs reflect this equality of the two sexes. Jesus has come to teach the divine law, Joan has asserted it by its liberators.

"3. Liberty of conscience remains among us entire.

"4. We affirm reincarnation into various existences as indispensible for the education of humans, which correspond between them, even after death.

"5. Expiation is proportionate to one's faults, for none are eternally damned.

"6. Cruelty towards animals, those humans in formation, is a crime; it is their brethren that they strike.

"7. The final reward is promised to all the just, interdependent and devoted beings."

"If I am not mistaken, what is particular in your cult is the divinization of the woman and the communication with spirits?"

"Yes, monsieur; the woman has been, since the beginning, horribly slandered. It is necessary to rectify the legend of the apple: Heva and Adama knew sublime happiness when the spirit of sin took hold of the husband. He wanted to travel. After several months, they caught sight of a vast, magnificent land beyond an arm of the sea. 'Oh!' said Adam, 'the beautiful fruits! Let us taste them.' - 'I beg you, have nothing to do with them,' replied his wife, 'the Lord would grow angry.' Instead of responding, the husband set Heva upon his shoulders, and together they rejoiced on the isle with that perfidious dessert. God then said to the woman: 'You have sinned only by love; into your midst will descend the messiahs of Love who will redeem you, and you yourself will be the Messiah...'"

I rise while smiling. The little stove threw up a flame. I saw through the window the roof-tops of the houses bathed in the crepuscular sun. It was a very pure and gentle feast of rays, white clouds, slender chimneys, and I thought that the nouveau Essenism resembled this Parisian evening, that it was a little too much a fifth floor religion, not close enough to the earth, too much in the heavens!

·

THE GNOSTICS

From my worktable, I believe I hear knocking at my door. The din ceased when behind me someone pronounced: "It is the Aeon Jesus himself who, in 1887, laid hands on me and consecrated me bishop of Montségur." I turned around: "You are no doubt M. Doinel, the new Valentinus." - "So you say," resumes the apparition.

It is unnecessary to give to this dialog the least intention of irony. M. Jules Doinel, archivist at Orleans, is the most scholarly and most modest of men. No one investigates more deeply into Hellenic and Albigensian antiquity through the intellect and, what is better, through the heart. But I have wished to set down in a clear tract forthwith the lofty and candid impression of the legend left by the Gnostic Patriarch, president of the Holy Synod of the "Perfect" and the "Pure."

"Do you know why we suffer and are so often evil?" the Apostle asked me. "The Demiurge - not God himself - created the world. This Demiurge, poor worker in the service of Sophia, the soul of the universe fallen by her noble desire to know too much, made us in his own image, too little beautiful; but Sophia took pity. By her will, a tear from herself and from heaven inhabited our clay. The Demiurge avenged himself by binding man to the flesh, from which he will be delivered only through the knowledge of his destiny, through *Gnosis*. The history of the soul, thrall of the impurities of the body, then soaring up even unto divine immortality, resides entirely in the legend of that sublime courtesan, Ennoia-Helene, companion of Simon Magus, become Goddess, and having her lover become

God through faith in the Eternal Feminine.

"Gnosticism repels any alliance with anti-Christian philosophy, be it Buddhist, Hindu, or occult. It turns away with horror from that Satanic magic of which the talent of M. Huysmans has just painted the picture and the process in his book entitled 'Là-bas.'

"It is not pantheistic. It acknowledges the personality in the unity, the identity in the fusion with God. Like the ocean rolls into its depths the droplets of water which remain *themselves* all while being it."

Science of the Theophanies and of the apparitions of the Divine.

Open eyes of the Lord over the shadow of the deserts;
Spirits which fill the air, water, and earth;
Angels of all names; mysterious phantoms,
Whose invisible world is fuller than atoms;
Holy ministers of the Father in all living places,
Who shines in the fire, who passes in the wind,
Invisible witness of our terrestrial hatreds.

Lamartine.

"The Gnosis," said Ephrem the Syrian, "wreathes a crown upon all those who love her, and she seats him upon the throne of the king."

There are three ascending classes among the Gnostics: the *Hylics*, still devoted to the preponderance of the flesh; the *Psychics*, among whom the soul awakens; the *Pneumatics*, who communicate with the Paraclete, being themselves already Spirit.

Three sacraments: the *Consolamentum*, a laying on of

hands and a kiss - the baptism of the Albigensians; the *Breaking of the Bread*, symbolic sacrifice where the astral body of Jesus descends; the *Appareillamentum*, reunion with grace, reserved to the patriarch alone.

The Gnostic clergy, formed of many priests and Catholic prelates, is composed of bishops and My Lady, deacons and deaconesses, a patriarch or a terrestrial Sophia. This latter man or woman wears the silver ring which is set with an amethyst; his gloves are violet, the Tau is suspended from his neck by a violet silk cord. The habit is adorned with a small cloak.

A canticle, the harmony of which has the purity of flax, opens the rite of worship. I give it, poem readers, in French as well as in Latin:

Bienheureux, vous, les Eons, (Blessed are you, the Aeons,)
Vivaces de la vrais vie, (Tenacious of the true life,)
Vous, emanations (You, emanations)
Du plérôme lucide, (Of the lucid pleroma,)
Soyez présentes, visions (Be present, visions)
Candides sous vos étoles blanche! (Candid under your white stoles!)

Beati vos Eones
Vera vita vividi,
Vos emanaitones
Pleromatis lucidi;
Adeste visiones,
Stolis albis candidi.

Here again in French is the first couplet from the

hymn to the Holy Pleroma:

> Saint, salut, royaume (Hail, holy kingdom)
> D'eternelle clarté. (Of eternal clarity.)
> Salut, salut, Plérôme, (Hail, hail, Pleroma)
> De la divinité! (Of the divinity!)
> Abime! O mer immense (Abyss! O immense sea)
> Où meut la substance. (Where substance stirs.)
> Mystère de silence, (Mystery of silence,)
> D'amour et de beauté. (Love, and beauty.)

A table covered only by an unsullied cloth, that is the Altar. Two flambeaux keep watch here over the Gospel of Saint John, patron of the sect. First of all they state the Pater while kneeling; then the officiant rises, holding the cup and the bread enveloped in a spotless linen, blesses it with three fingers, Gnostically, and exclaims: *Touto esti, touto soma*; for the Greek mixes with this delicate rite its scholarly grace. Toward the faithful he turns himself, exhorts them to confess their sins publicly, like the first Christians; and if they repent, their sins are remitted. Finally, he invites the most worthy to eat the body and drink the cup of the blood of the Aeon Christ.

This is clear: the new Gnosticism, like the old, attempts to establish a sort of aristocracy within Catholicism, with its eyes too material, too vulgarized.

Thus, the first act of the Holy Synod was to grant the Consolamentum to the Abbé Roca, that the Roman Church, when he died, rejected from its bosom. Valentin gathered in spirit, at eight-thirty in the evening , the Grand Assembly, composed of the bishops of Montségur, Toulouse, Béziers, Avignon, the coadjutor of His Grace the patriarch, bishop of Milan, the coadjutor of Toulouse, bishop of Concorezzo, and Her Ladyship the Sophia. All, at the same moment, lay on hands and utter the evocation by which the astral envelope of the deceased is to be blessed and delivered.

In 1891, a special report was addressed to the Holy Office against the resurrection of Albigensian and Cathar Gnosticism. Therein they indicated to the Pope two dangers: the one which threatens the faith, the rebirth of the *dualist* and *emanationist* heresy; the other which threatens the hierarchy, the reconstitution of the episcopate and the Gnostic assembly with a definite episcopal see: *Montségur*. *Ama et fac quod vis*! Such is the motto of the new Elect. How is to be described this chivalric and so romantic heresy, of which Dante and Escarmonde were the most glorious pontiffs? Such purity and mystery would demand the inspiration of a poet of the Silence, like M. Rodenbach, the immaculate language of the snow, the calm waves, lowered eyes, and mirrors.

THE CULT OF ISIS

Isis decidedly emerged from her Egyptian ruins. She emigrated from the sarcophagi and the museums in order to inhabit the minds of the intellectuals and the hearts of discreet faithful. The memorable day is near when will be re-established, on a neighboring hillside, her temple and her initiation by the cares of some adept, a woman no doubt, reincarnating the Goddess according to the dream of the melancholic prophet Villiers de l'Isle-Adam.

Madame the Duchess of Pomar has dreamed, I am told, as one instance, that they could believe her to be the terrestrial Sophia of the Gnostics. What say I? M. Dubut de Laforest, until then little suspected of extremist idealism, neophyte touched by grace, was converted. In the preface of a novel on business people, he praised the religious efforts of Isiac resurrection that Auguste Comte began and that Jules Michelet has blessed[12].

Isis has her world-class painters like Antoine de La Rochefoucauld, who considered her the sister of Sophia and of the Ennoia of the Pleroma; she has her poets, her sculptors, her song-writers too, the sentimental Boukay.

But it was reserved to the *Revue des Deux Mondes* to bear upon this doctrine and these rites moving revelations. By a magisterial work, le Masque, M. Gilbert- Augustin Thierry, life-long occultist, writer of subtle pages on the "Second Life" and Expiation, synthesized the awakening at Paris of these mysteries; and from the heights of Montmartre radiates over the City "the Reincarnation of Isis," those *salutistes* of a most noble spirit.

"It is not a dream of my imagination," my learned

interlocuter explained to me; "rather, an intellectual desire. Student of Proclus, Plotinus, Porphyry, Iamblicus, the greatest of the Cæsars of Rome expiring , Julian was our precursor. Origen too, who formulated not only 'metempsychosis,' that is to say the transfusion of the soul into inferior husks, but 'metensomatosis,' the transmission of our spirit into successive human bodies. Ancient Egypt had already made of this dogma the basis of its social morals. For the evil and the wretched, there is no eternal torture; all must be reborn according to the moral state that their past life has placed them, make amends, and purify themselves until attaining God.

"Ecstasy - Enose - that is the true method to unite the creature to the creator. There, where reason stops, the heart still soars; he who can go so far as sacrifice and martyrdom.

"Isis is Goodness, the Heart, the whole doctrine. What religion is preferable? Alexandria, Italy, Africa, old Gaul, unto its most remote ruins, have kept the remembrance thereof. On the side of the hill, since named Sainte-Geneviève hill, recent excavations around the basilica of Saint-Germain-des-Près uncovered a statue of a woman holding a child in her arms. The clergy believed they were seeing a Virgin Mary. She operated miracles; but the archeologists later having recognized it as an Isis, she was expelled from the sanctuary as demoniacal. What shall I tell you on the most modern cult of the Goddess? A stamp from the year VII depicts an Isiac ceremony designed by 'citizens, friends, and zealots of the good Goddess.' The production conforms to the description of the initiatic ceremonies, the splendor of which book XI of the Metamorphoses of Apuleus relates minutely. Maxime Du

Camp and Louis Bouihet worshipped Isis, preceded by Cagliostro who, in the last century, instituted his initiation among the ladies of the court."

What has charmed me in M. Gilbert-Augustin Thierry, is that he cannot be accused of founding a religion. Not a pontiff, a spiritualist writer, a Neoplatonic philosopher, a sage. While I listened to him, I seemed to hear, if not a reincarnation of Hermes, at least some Apuleus pouring forth, in an eloquent tongue, the marvels of a Milesian tale.

Also have I found him very hard on the spiritists, too hard even. I know, among the believers in metensomatosis, fierce and tender souls who deserve a lauditory citation: I wish to speak of M. Bouvery and of the poets René Caillié and Camille Chaigneau.

Could the cult of Isis be one of the most attractive forms of renascent spiritualism, drenched in the irreproachable experiments of a scientist such as Richet, and all radiant with the tenderness of future women? In any case, it sums up, in the distaste for dying naturalisms, the anxiety of the age towards beyond austere unto chastity, and human unto the tears of the Mother[13].

ISIS, THE ETERNAL CULT OF GOODNESS[14]
I

The history of Egypt teaches us the art of governing men while not letting them be led toward either of those two sorrowful and deadly poles which are called: in the north Despotism, in the south Anarchy[15]!

To say that the equilibrium always remains perfect, would be to go much too far and to demand the impossible from a land inhabited, after all, by men. To say that the tendency of Egypt was not toward a certain attraction to that pole of the north that we have named Despotism, glacial pole among us, would be to defy history itself, to disfigure time. But that, for thousands of years, the government maintained itself in magnificent rigidity, we must declare it with joy and applaud on this occasion the esoteric science which permits this miracle;... is not this persistence for so long of one same principle of authority a miracle for us, moderns, who change ministers like clothes, and who are ignorant of the shortest stability of power?

The adventurers, the arbitrary sovereignties, the brutal Assyrian dynasties united in league against the strong and tranquil Egypt, where the old order had not been troubled.

Fortunately, its priesthood was not a simple primary school imposing submission upon the multitudes and leaving the governors without any other control than their good pleasure and their ignorance; far from it. Knowledge, wisdom - initiation, in a word, solidly seated and defended in the enormous temples of Thebes, prolonged its beneficent influence over the people by the intermediary of the pharaohs born from them.

The people were and believed whatever they wanted. Outside of the first degree of instruction and professional education, outside of the cult of the ancestors, nothing was imposed upon them, although all was accessible to them according to their will[16].

It is always the same in all times, the multitude may take the signs for the things signified, the symbols for the causes, the hieroglyphs for the cosmogonic powers, the princes for the principles, the priests and the cult itself for the religion and the truth[17].

But even among the disinherited, the teachings of the soul were excellent, though the symbols were not scientifically explained to all.

Each possessed precise, though rudimentary, notions on the visible and invisible life; a sacred scroll, containing a sublime confession of faith, was piously kept by the adult until his death, and accompanied him even unto the life beyond the tomb, admirably known, revered, and supported by the living of these temples.

As to the pharaohs, they donned the insignia of command only after having been severely and for a long time instructed in the royal art, that is to say set straight by a formidable intellectual and moral discipline that our military schools, our universities, and even our seminaries, our convents, could not call upon.

If we see, at certain periods, the kings succeed one another to the throne with such rapidity, it is because mediocrity and governmental deviation was not long tolerated by the initiatic colleges, who would rather support at their own expense the more or less disordered life of an idle prince than to leave him outside and a sovereignty over others that he did not have within himself.

Ah! the business of a pharaoh was not the business of a lazy king; Egypt was occupied to the extreme, it kept the whole world going, not only in war, but in peace, for its trades consumed the premiere materials of three continents, of which the Phoenecians were the maritime carriers.

Outside of the temples, the pharaoh was everywhere, on all sides.

Supreme magistrate, head of the army, head of the scholarly body, ever faithful to the ancient tradition, grand for its time, immense for our own, he bore upon his shoulders duties of a frightful weight. He also leaned over the gulf which attracts power towards his own ruin and inclining him to become egotistical.

But in the temples where the priesthood was with him, the king represented his true blood in the true hierarchy; he was no more than an initiate, and nearly always of the first degree.

Kneeling on both knees, head bare, stripped of all arms, he piously took the chalice and the sacred bread that the high priest offered him; then he heard lessons other than the titillation of the disguised flatteries of Boussuet: "God alone is great, my brethren!" In his place, in his stall, he listened to the voice of the prophets performing the sacred rites, evoking the living soul of the ancestors, dictating their teachings to their royal listener, reproving him on the past or the present, if there was cause, and tracing out his future if his response to their questioning was insufficient.

These days when we see personages so little instructed on the things of the heart and the spirit, presumptuously claiming power and speaking on the master; when, on the other hand, we hear arise from the midst of the laborious and oppressed classes the great cries of all the hunger and thirst; if suddenly we transport ourselves into that remote past we recognize how little wisdom resides from top to bottom; but it is not to man, ever barbarous in his avidity and egotistical in his ambitions, it is not to man such as our overheated and incomplete civilization made him that is restored the right and the duty to govern his equals, but to the one who, on the contrary, has stripped himself of vile concupiscences, dominating instincts, to the one who is at once a sage, a scholar, a devotee. And this one shall have authority only by the delegation of his peers or his superiors; he must in the light of day divest himself of all pride and prestige in order to listen, before the tribunal of his elders, to the praise or blame, to counsel.

In Egypt, the direction of the government belonged, in reality, to the initiation; but the initiation was open to every one, except of course that it was more difficult for the great than for the humble; all the more harsh as the individual ascended the degrees leading to the most serious responsibilities.

Is this not an echo of that superb initiatic law which, it seems to me, is well made to be pleasing in our day to the spirits displaced by injustices of fate and of the stupid inequality of fortunes; is it not an echo of that law that the words of Jesus Christ later asserted, how it is difficult for the rich and powerful to arrive at what he calls the kingdom of his Father, that is to say at supreme knowledge?

Jesus Christ always asserted that the simplicity of the heart and the simplification of the spirit are the fundamental conditions of knowledge and true happiness[18]. Their symbol is the child. "Let come to me the little children; truly, I say "to you, if you do not become like little children, you will not enter the kingdom of heaven."

Here then, is the ideal theory of government by the initiates; I indicate only the summary schema thereof: at the bottom the masses, at the top is initiation; between initiation and the masses, the men of government arising from initiation after having dwelled with the masses; in summary, an organic society like a living being with an abdomen, a head, and arms.

If Egypt preserved for so long its power and its unity, it is because this governmental principle was in it; if it perished, it is because it no longer obeyed. This is what happened: the initiates, instead of renewing themselves among the people, sought to succeed one another, from father to son. The pharaohs, on the other hand, more and more intoxicated by their military victories, sought to extricate themselves from the influence of the initiates and to recruit in these people soldiers or slave workers. The people became brutalized or revolted. There was no longer within this powerful organism of Egyptian society the regular movement of the circulation of blood; the abdomen grew heavy, the arms contracted in a gesture of authority, the head became hazy by literal science and prideful darkness.

II

What charlatanic pretension to wish for all the pieces to reconstruct the esoteric doctrine taught by the Egyptian priesthood!

The Hermetic books which seemed at first the perfect manual, are not authentic and date, for the editing at least, to the neo-Alexandrians. Did Hermes even exist? The God Thoth, of which he is the Greek translation, served to designate a caste of men preoccupied with legislating the mysteries. There was such beauty in the science and arts of Egypt, that they wished to remain anonymous. The Pharaohs have left for us their names, but the artists, the scholars, the philosophers, they practiced an absolute discretion. Thus has the sacrifice of the personality of the worker made the work immortal. We do not know the name of the architect of the Great Pyramid, of the sculptor of the Sphinx of Giza, no more than we can attribute a precise name to the *Pymander*, those few divine pages, of the *Book of the Dead*, which is the highest revelation which has been given to us on the beyond! In this way yet, our paltry and egoist time remains well at fault; our artists, our writers, our sages, are preoccupied before all with having a good crowd and leaving to their posterity a resounding fame. But what remains of these isolated and vain efforts? Man alone can do nothing; the solitude is pride - the pride is nothingness and ruin.

I am going to attempt then, thanks to the papyri, to the hieroglyphs, to the statues, to the monuments, to extirpate from Egypt its mystery; it spoke its austere and logical language, but I cannot, alas, but transmit to you very few syllables and some effaced sounds.

What results, in sum, from that slow and painful inquiry? It is that Egypt expressed and explained the theory of Goodness.

Certainly, Egypt is the blessed land *par excellence*. The arid and burning desert right next to it made it by contrast an oasis. The water drew the thirsty populations; the Nile offers itself to them, the benevolent and fecondating Nile. The Nile does not deceive; its regularity, similar to that of the stars, quickly gave to this primitive people the sense of the law, the idea of a God! It has the pontifical exactitude of the Sun. Both are sure and benevolent fathers; nothing capricious, deceitful , or fallible. Men venerate and adore them; both are Ammon-Ra or Osiris. They represent the male principle which, by a double kiss, that of light and that of water, inseminates the maternal earth, the good Isis, so obedient and so fertile, that from which the inexhaustible breast pours out to its children the inexhaustible milk of the Gods.

It is not terror which, in Egypt, invents the divinity, as they might believe for the people of the North, persecuted by nature, victims of the dangers of the forest and avalanches. It is, on the contrary, the thankfulness which lets God be found in man! Now, God is good; man, therefore, shall be good. All of Egypt, in its heroic primitiveness, pushes toward Heaven and earth a hymn of confidence and grave joy. "Give yourself to the divinity," say the sacred Scriptures, "keep yourself constantly for the Divinity and that the next day be as today, that your eye gaze upon the acts of the Divinity." Further on are these phrases of a magnificent burst of tenderness: "It is I who has given you your mother, but it is she who has carried you, and in carrying you she has had many back pains to suffer, and she has not unloaded them upon me. You are born after months of pregnancy, and she has carried you as a veritable yoke, her breast in your mouth, for three years. You gained strength, and the repugnance of your dirtiness has not disgusted her to the point of making her say: 'Oh! what shall I do?' You were put in school; while they instructed you in the scriptures, she was each day diligent with your teacher, bringing him bread and drink from home. You have arrived at adult age, you are married, you have taken a household. Never lose sight of the painful child birth that you have cost your mother, all the salutary care that, she has taken of you. Do not do what she might complain about you, for fear that she raises her hands to the divinity and that this latter might hear her complaints."

The great cult of Egypt is definitively the cult of Isis, the cult of the Universal Mother! This reasonable and moved land was not heresiarchal in this sense, for it recognized, as her equal, the male principle Osiris; but it reserved its whole heart to the sacred feminine, to Nature which gives birth, like the Mother, like Isis. Thus does an immense goodness hover over this religion which appears at first so multiform, so incoherent, so bestial. The vaunt therein "the patient suffering of man"; are they not all fragments of that excellent Osiris, who, in order to create human beings, dispersed his members? "Ammon-Ra makes the grasses push forth for the beasts, the plants for the men, it is he who makes live the fish in the river, the birds in the sky and upon the branch; be blessed for all this, Unique, Multiple of arms." A naive song, but impregnated with faith!

Consequently, an exquisite morality.

"Do not save your life at the cost of that of others, it is prescribed; give food to those who hunger, drink to those who thirst, clothing to the one who is naked, and a boat to the one who is stopped in his route." Or again these resigned and clement words where experience smiles: "Have we ever seen a place where there is no rich or poor? But the bread remains with the one who acts fraternally." There is, in the examination of conscience of the Egyptian who, purified, presents himself after death to the tribunal of Osiris, a particularly sublime word: it seems to me to synthesize the entire morality of these strong and delicate souls. After having enumerated the good that he has been able to do in life, the deceased adds:

"I have never made anyone cry."

I do not know any more ineffable, virtuous flower to breathe.

This goodness would degenerate into an infantile weakness. The plant and even the animal become for man companions, friends, I was going to say equals. But I could not yet express here but a small part of the truth: the people bowed before them as before their superiors; it was the same with the Gods. The infallible instinct of the animals which announces the return of the seasons struck this observant people, and from here to granting them a divine prescience, there was only one step; an error touching and fecond in reflections! Christianity and refined philosophy were shocked. A Father of the Church wrote: "Do you know what the God of Egypt is? An impure beast, sprawled upon a purple cloth." Later, Bossuet condemned without call: "In Egypt, all was God, except God himself." The esoteric priests supported with more patience the popular idolatry; they saw therein an homage too material, it is true, but an homage nevertheless to the immaterial divinity who made use of matter as a cloak which poorly indicates his impeccable presence! Then, they did not know, like the Initiates, from time immemorial, that man has formed progressively upon this planet, that the force of the Universe is one, and that it is by a slow selection, through a difficult evolution across imperfect forms that he has finally appeared, the most beautiful terrestrial symbol of the invisible Divinity. Every Egyptologist even slightly distinguished, M. Maspero, M. Pierrot, or M. Geuzer, or M. Lenormant, admits today that it is the Egyptian priesthood whence Moses emerged, the monotheist believing in One God. Those innumerable statues of divinities with the bodies of men and the heads of beasts intend to express the different functions, the various attributes of the Supreme God, like, in return, each stage of the sun in its celestial or infernal course corresponds to a stage of the existence of man. One text is, moreover, definitive: "We do not carve Gods," it is proclaimed therein, "in stone, in the statues upon which we place the double crown; God does not see it, we do not know the place where he is."

But if the Initiates leave the vulgar to plunge themselves into that incomplete truth of the uniquely material evolution where are limited our modern Darwinists, they, enlarging the law, apply it also to the souls and spirits. They believe in that shower of souls falling from the faraway sun across the planets upon the miserable earth, law of divine involution, corresponding to the law of terrestrial evolution; and this shower of souls fallen from Osiris, they see then re-forming into a sort of jet which, emerging from the very depths of the earth, are going to plunge, by passing ever through the planets, into the heart of the sun.

Even the densest "exoteric" doctrine is but a veil, under which trembles, luminous, the "esoteric" truth, discernable for the attentive spirit of goodwill.

We are departing from the exoteric doctrine of the easily graspable popular ideas, in order to raise ourselves unto the esoteric philosophy that we are going to formulate very simply in three aphorisms:

1.   The law of goodness which asserts itself from itself in the heart of man, lets him discover the universal fraternity across the hierarchy of beings.

2.   That fraternity is supported upon a double law of evolution and involution, law by which, while God descends and folds himself back into the Universe, the Universe ascends and unfolds itself toward God.

3. Therefore, before impartial eyes, nothing is small, nothing is great, or rather the great equals the small, the without is like the within, the vegetable like the animal, the animal like man, man like God, the visible like the invisible, life like death.

Be blessed, holy Isis, bloody mother, you who have suffered so that it is permitted to forgive you. You remain the sole divinity who will save the world. You were the promise of the Messiah of Love, you announced, before Jesus, the Paraclete. Being pure woman but ever burning with the experiences of life, you efface the feeble Virgin, the Mary of the sorrowful Church. There you are, O Pacificatrix of the people, the Goddess of universal redemption, the Queen of Life and Death, the Best and most beautiful; O Creatrix of the invincible certitudes - There you are above misled intelligences, the Heart.

ENDNOTES

1. It is necessary to cite towards the end of the eighteenth century Quintus Aucher who attempted to restore a Neoplatonic, gnostic, and occultist paganism; he wished for the ancient pagan holidays to be observed and called Jupiter the Sacred Quaternary by which all exists and which moves nature. Quintus Aucher has written, to the glory of the Gods, the *Threicie*. In our day, M.L.P., senator, author of the less unknowns and old editor of the "Nouvelle Revue," renders homage in his apartments to his protector genius an idol of Athena.

2. I received a letter from M. the pastor Décembre which asserts his church "The New Jerusalem" to be independent of all evocatory mysticism and based upon the texts of the two Testaments, commented upon by Swedenborg. How I regret the Huguenot and positivist turn of this little religion, so inspired and so strange in its extraordinary founder!

3. "Knowledge alone, not faith," M. de Milloué writes to me, but who, what will give to the scholar the courage to labor for knowledge, if not faith?

4. The rite of this sect is impregnated with a delicate mysticism and a faith in the divine supernatural from which all stray, other Buddhists in fact.
    M. de Bonnières who, in the *Baiser de Maina*, evoked with the eyes of a witness and the intuition of a poet, Bénarès la Ville Sainte, explained to me these

profound differences by the diversity of the
"vehicles" and the wholly other comprehension of
the doctrine of the Buddha by the literal materialists
of the South and the mystics of the North.

5. Principle of vitality, the second according to the
seven-fold division established by the Hindu
occultists.

6. I furnish a complete study of Vintrasism in my
book: *Le Satanisme et la Magie.*

7. Would the Prayer to the Mystery therefore end all
profound philosophy at the career of every upright
man? A striking particularity that certain disciples
sought to conceal, at least to mitigate, but which is
revealed, irresistible charm for the souls who prefer
the naiveties of the heart to the refinements of
intelligence.

8. It was decided by Providence that the strongest
head of this century would restore the most delicate
and immaterial of cults: that of the Woman and of
the Virgin Mother, mediatrix between the Great
Being and its pontiffs; of the one who, divine
indeed, carries, against her chaste breast, the Child.

9. An Englishman used to come each year to make his
devotions at the chamber of Auguste Comte; his
name: Mr. James C. Morison, collaborator at the
Fortnightly Review, and author of works appreciated
by Louis XIV and William of Orange; he arrived at
Paris accompanied by his wife, even more devoted,
if possible, to the "cult of humanity."

10. It is to be noted that we owe to a Jesuit the best
work done on the work and person of Auguste
Comte.

11. If there is some heaviness in the exposé of this admirable system, my readers should refer to Auguste Comte that I have cited nearly verbatim; the spiritual wings of this genius did not prevent a certain unwieldiness of style.

12. A madman - for madness poisons the most noble new attempts - M. Mazaroz, furniture dealer, proclaimed, deforming the pure religion of Isis, the cult of the genital parts of the woman. Through the keenness of perspicacious chronicles, M. Paul Foucher, in the *Gil Blas*, burst this impure balloon.

13. M. the doctor Baraduc, who studies and tests the vital fluid, is in this point the scientist of the Terrestrial Isis, soul of the universe and men.

14. Extract from the *Cours d'occultsime* by M. Jules Bois (1893).

15. I have already explained many times that Initiation requires a sort of anarchy with the obedience to God, to his impersonal laws, but that it feels repugnance toward that other anarchy which is but the slavery of the coarse passions.

16. This is counter to the castes of India which were too quickly closed, then ossified.

17. I condense and complete here a magnificent chapter by the Marquis de Saint-Yves d'Alveydre on Egypt.

18. And not the Knowledge and Happiness in itself, as has asserted M. de Wyzewa, who, moreover, has confused simplicity with stupidity and simplification with ignorance.

www.ingramcontent.com/pod-product-compliance
Lightning Source LLC
Chambersburg PA
CBHW020920090426
42736CB00008B/727